The Winners

Sydney 2000
Olympic
Games

PENGUIN BOOKS

Produced with the assistance of The Sydney Morning Herald

Contents

The publisher would like to acknowledge the contribution of the following:

Allsport (photographs)
Murray Olds (sports reports)

Features

Results

And the winner is…Sydney!

Sydney's famous icons dressed for the occasion

After seven years of intense preparation, it was time for Sydney to host the first major sporting event of the new millennium. Everyone willed Sydney to sparkle and their hopes were surpassed many times over.

For the first week, day after day dawned with cloudless blue skies. When rain eventually came, however, it did nothing to dampen the Olympic spirit and the crowds remained huge and supportive. The transport system ran like a well-oiled machine, moving some 16 million people with ease, on some days transporting over 400 000 spectators to and from Olympic Park.

Sydney and its people embraced the games with a pure enjoyment that was infectious. It was party time in Sydney and everyone joined in enthusiastically. The city brimmed with colour, life and excitement. Lights twinkled in the trees, the sails of the Opera House were bathed in a myriad of colours, and the Olympic rings burned brightly on the Harbour Bridge. People flocked to Olympic Live sites around the city, willing the athletes to go faster, higher and stronger. Dozens of world records were set with the

Millennium Athlete, the official logo for the Sydney Olympic Games

crowd support lifting competitors to new levels. Several of the events gave Sydney a brilliant opportunity to showcase its natural and man-made assets: beach volleyball at Bondi, the triathlon around the Opera House, and sailing on the picturesque Sydney Harbour gave visitors a chance to see Sydney in all its glory.

In the intense enthusiasm and support for the locals, the chant of 'Aussie, Aussie, Aussie …' reverberated around many of the sporting venues; happily at the same time the sports-mad Australian crowds also recognised the true achievements of all participating nations.

Much of the credit for the success of the Games has to go to the 47 000-strong army of tireless volunteers who guided, assisted and organised the sea of humanity by undertaking thousands of duties on the streets of Sydney. They went about their jobs with a friendliness that left a lasting impression on both visitors and locals.

The international response was unanimous, full of praise for the city that had got it right! The organisers of the Salt Lake City Winter Olympics (to be held in 2002) were 'genuinely stunned' by how smoothly everything ran. Singapore's *Straits Times* ran a front-page headline: 'Good on ya'. *Time* described a 'beaming Australia' and ran the headline: 'The land down under on top of the world'. *La Parisienne* waxed: 'These Games are wonderful. Australia has put on a Games for the world'. *Sports Illustrated* wrote: 'Sydney. Let's make it official. Sydney is now the Olympics' permanent home. Let Sydney take care of 2004 ... I'm serious. Sydney 2008'. A journalist on United States public radio captured the Sydney 2000 Olympic spirit perfectly: 'These are the friendliest people you could imagine. That's what I'll remember of these Games'. With professionalism, a smile and a score of perfect ten, Sydney had delivered the greatest show on earth.

Obliging volunteers were there to help visitors at every turn

Stadium Australia, filled to the brim with enthusiastic spectators

The Olympic Torch Relay

Kindled by the rays of the sun in Olympia, Greece, the Olympic flame travelled 36 600 kilometres and through thirteen countries to begin its inspiring Australian journey at Uluru. The flame is the heart of the Olympic spirit, and the great rock in the red centre is the heart of Australia. On 8 June, the Governor-General, Sir William Deane, lit the torch of the first runner, the first indigenous Australian to win an Olympic gold medal, Nova Peris-Kneebone. A journey of 100 days, to the opening of the Sydney 2000 Olympic Games, had begun.

At the start of its 27 000-kilometre odyssey, the longest ever, the Torch Relay was only a whisper. But from near and far they came to hear the voice of symbolism and meaning. Even on the remote Nullarbor, towns with populations in single digits suddenly swelled to thousands, and in every State and Territory, 'look at all the people' became a constant refrain. Everywhere the Torch went, Australians seemed to hear its call grow louder.

The Torch, carried here through the Barossa Valley, brought the spirit of the Games to regional Australia

It was just a tiny flicker of light, but incredibly its route passed close to nearly 90 per cent of Australia's total population of 19 million people. It was carried by young and old, ordinary Australians and heroes, athletes, Olympians past and present,

people of every race, culture and creed who now call Australia their home. It was carried on horseback, by the Royal Flying Doctor air service and on the Indian Pacific railway. It travelled underwater at the Great Barrier Reef, and through snowfields, tropics and deserts. In cities or the country, everyone who saw it experienced an Olympic moment they would remember all their lives. Spectator numbers grew beyond all imagining, and by the time the Torch reached Sydney its voice had become a mighty roar.

Hundreds of thousands of people poured into the streets of the host city to welcome the Torch. On the 99th day, when it reached the city's great icons, the Opera House and Harbour Bridge, the tiny flickering flame transformed Sydney into 'The City of Light'–the Olympic Rings shone brightly on the Bridge, and the lights of the city's buildings added to the spectacle.

At the end of an expedition that took 100 days and involved 11 000 runners, 110 000 people packed into Stadium Australia and 4 billion viewers tuned in around the world, with just one question on their lips: Who would carry the Torch on the last leg of its awesome journey to the Olympic Games?

Crowds followed the Torch wherever it went

3

The Opening Ceremony

Cathy Freeman, 400-metre athletics world champion, had the honour of lighting the cauldron

It began with a lone rider galloping into the centre of the stadium, rearing on his stockhorse and cracking his stockwhip. It was a true Australian call to attention, and the world listened. What followed was almost sixty minutes of drama, colour and spectacle. 'The Man from Snowy River' was then joined by 120 riders on horses, bearing Olympic flags. Majestic and en masse, they formed a guard of honour as the Australian National Anthem was sung by Julie Anthony and Human Nature.

The history of the host nation then unfolded in seven cultural sequences, as seen through the eyes of black and white Australia. Linking each vision was 13-year-old Nikki Webster, guided through the ages by tribal Aboriginal Djakapurra Munyarryun, in the true spirit of reconciliation. *Deep Sea Dreaming* turned the stadium into the Great Barrier Reef, with sea creatures scurrying across the ocean floor while giant colourful fish and swimmers navigated the waters above. *Awakening* brought together hundreds of Aboriginal and

The rainbow of participating nations

Torres Strait Islander dancers, while the fragrance of burning gum leaves filled the stadium. Then a spectacular depiction of *Fire* spread across the arena, spurring *Nature* into renewal as Australian wildflowers bloomed in a riot of colour. The advent of the Europeans followed, with the first settlers arriving in the stadium. The *Tin Symphony* brought larrikins, Ned Kelly figures and corrugated iron sheds as white Australia made its mark on the land. Then there was a whimsical touch when a legion of lawnmowers fired up – as they do every weekend in suburban backyards across Australia – to form the Olympic rings. With *Arrivals*, the peoples of Africa, Asia, Europe and the Americas converged in a celebration of Australia's multiculturalism. This was followed by a tribute to Australian workers: hundreds of tap-dancers in Blundstones and flannelette shirts constructed a Harbour Bridge emblazoned with the word *Eternity*.

The Australians, led by Andrew Gaze, captain of the men's basketball team and five-time Olympian

Then it was the turn of the 2000-strong Olympic Marching Band made up of musicians from twenty countries. They created one of the greatest massed-band spectacles ever and welcomed the Olympic athletes as they entered the stadium. History was made as a tiny team from East Timor marched in as 'Individual Olympic Athletes' and North and South Korea marched together for the first time behind one flag.

Australian women's hockey captain Rechelle Hawkes took the athletes' oath and the Governor-General, Sir William Deane, declared the Games open. In a tribute to 100 years of participation by women in the modern Olympics, the Torch was carried in a final relay by seven of Australia's greatest female athletes: Raelene Boyle and Betty Cuthbert, Dawn Fraser, Shirley Strickland de la Hunty, Shane Gould, Debbie Flintoff-King, and, finally, Cathy Freeman. The audience roared its approval as Freeman walked to the centre of a reflective pool, touched the Torch to its surface and water became fire. The cauldron emerged from the pool and rose to the top of the stadium. The Games of the XXVII Olympiad had begun.

Djakapurra Munyarryun and Nikki Webster: two cultures, ancient and youthful, hand in hand

Raelene Boyle and Betty Cuthbert with the Olympic Torch

Aquatics

Diving

Drought broken

Synchronized diving was a new event at the Sydney Olympic Games. The atmosphere was electrifying as Australian duo Rebecca Gilmore and Loudy Tourky needed a big score, with a single dive remaining, in the **women's 10-metre platform synchronized**.

Rebecca Gilmore and Loudy Tourky (AUS) win Australia's first medal in diving since 1924

They were in fourth place behind the Austrians, but with the crowd on its feet supporting them, they came up with the goods. The two executed a sensational back two-and-a-half somersault with half twist to take the bronze. It was Australia's first diving medal since Dick Eve took gold in 1924 in the plain high diving competition. Li Na and Sang Xue (CHN) always had the gold medal in the bag; Emilie Heymans and Anne Montminy (CAN) finished second.

Faultless display

A faultless display by Xiao Hailiang and Xiong Ni (CHN), in the **men's 3-metre springboard synchronized**, delivered gold to China by a wide margin. It was the second gold medal of the competition for Xiong Ni, after his win in the **men's 3-metre springboard**. He was competing in his fourth Olympic Games. Third place in the **men's 3-metre springboard synchronized** went to Robert Newbery and Dean Pullar, as Australia picked up its second medal. The pair leapt into contention after an excellent fourth dive, a forward two-and-a-half somersault with two twists. It looked spectacular in the air, and the pair hit the water together.

Xiong Ni (CHN) heads for gold in the men's 3-metre springboard

6   See Diving results on page 88.

≈ Swimming

Australia's dream start

Even swimming at world record pace, Ian Thorpe (AUS) looked as if he was on a training swim, his technique as calm as his smile. With the expectation of a nation riding on this first swim, he cruised the pool in the **men's 400-metre freestyle**, keeping just ahead of a worrying challenger, Massimiliano Rosolino (ITA). At 300 metres, though, 'Thorpedo' broke away, his legs and feet pumping in a surge that left all in his wake. He hit the wall in 3:40.59, just outside his own world record, lifted both fists in the air and mouthed the words 'thank you' – acknowledging the ecstatic crowd and the people close to him. It was a small prayer for a dream come true.

Ian Thorpe (AUS) clinches gold in the men's 400-metre freestyle

Finally, the wait is over

Distance swimmer Brooke Bennett (USA) had to wait four long years to make up for her shock failure to qualify in the Atlanta Games for the **women's 400-metre freestyle**. She won the 800 in Atlanta, but her personal burden was only lifted in Sydney when she easily won the 400 ahead of compatriot Diana Munz (USA). Bennett later won the **women's 800-metre freestyle** to move into the same realm of greatness as American swim

Brooke Bennett (USA) on her way to gold in the women's 800-metre freestyle

queen Janet Evans. The 20-year-old was only 1.95 seconds behind Evans's 1988 world record for the 400 and 3.45 seconds outside Evans's 800-metre record. She says these are the goals that will keep her swimming.

See Swimming results on pages 88–90.

Ian Thorpe
Swimming sensation

Ian Thorpe hates the public focus on his feet. But in a few short days in mid-September, he used those size-17 feet to leap into the hall of Australian sporting heroes, eclipsing the world's best swimmers and rewriting the record books.

Thorpe's long arms and legs, and his famous big feet, make him swim well, but it is hard work and attitude that have pushed him to the top of the world swimming heirarchy.

The 17-year-old took part in his first swimming carnival at 8 years of age; at 14 he was the youngest male swimmer to have qualified for the Australian team. At the 1998 world championships in Perth he became the youngest world champion when he won the 400-metre freestyle. His wonderful rhythmic style, his massive leg strength and power through the water showed then that there was a lot more to come.

His early years were spent in the Sydney suburb of Bankstown: swimming training, school work and a close-knit family life. His parents have not missed a carnival since Thorpe took up swimming and they were in the crowd in Sydney as he set Australia alight with his 400-metre freestyle win, his amazing final leg in the 4 x 100-metre freestyle relay and his work in the 4 x 200-metre freestyle relay success. They were equally supportive when he took silver in the 200-metre freestyle behind Pieter van den Hoogenband (NED).

Thorpe's words after that loss sum up his whole attitude to competition: 'It really was a privilege to be able to swim in that race'. Such a calm approach should enable him to realise his ambition to swim at two more Olympic Games. Amazingly, by then he will be only 25 years old.

Ian Thorpe (AUS) acknowledges the crowd after his win in the men's 400-metre freestyle

See Swimming results on pages 88–90.

Supercharged Italian

Italian Domenico Fioravanti came to Sydney as a relative unknown at breaststroke. He left as No. 1, having taken both the 100- and 200-metre titles, winning his country's first-ever gold medals in swimming. Like a supercharged Ferrari he won both races with his powerful finish. In the **men's 100-metre breaststroke** he surged from fifth place at the 50-metre mark and held off race favourites Ed Moses (USA) and world record holder Roman Sloudnov (RUS). Again in the **men's 200-metre breaststroke** he took the lead half way and kept the power turned on for a comfortable win. Terence Parkin (RSA) finished second and Davide Rummolo (ITA) third. Australia's Regan Harrison missed a bronze medal by only 0.15 seconds.

Domenico Fioravanti (ITA) and Davide Rummolo (ITA) celebrate their gold and bronze in the men's 200-metre breaststroke

Lethal Leisel

Leisel Jones (AUS) looked just what she was, a wide-eyed schoolgirl, as she lined up for the **women's 100-metre breaststroke** final. She was nervous, but came up smiling as she finished a touch behind Megan Quann (USA) for a silver medal.

In the **women's 200-metre breaststroke**, Hungarian teenager Agnes Kovacs broke Olympic records in her heat and semi-final, but looked in trouble in the final until she surged to snatch victory from Americans Kristy Kowal and Amanda Beard. Kovacs was 0.3 seconds outside her record of the previous night.

OLYMPIC FACT

Hungarian Agnes Kovacs has an ambition to match the five gold medals of her country's backstroke hero Krisztina Egerszegi, who was only the second woman to win the same event (100-metre backstroke) three times. Dawn Fraser was the first.

Leisel Jones (AUS), one of the most promising youngsters on the Australian swimming team

See Swimming results on pages 88–90.

The flying Dutchman

Pieter van den Hoogenband (NED) upset the swimming world order early in the meet when he edged out Australia's favourite son, Ian Thorpe, in the **men's 200-metre freestyle** after having broken Thorpe's world record in the heats. The two men turned for the last 50 metres in exactly the same time. It was surging pace against throbbing power, but the Dutchman won by equalling his own record time of 1:45.35. The crowd was momentarily stunned but then acknowledged the might of the Dutchman.

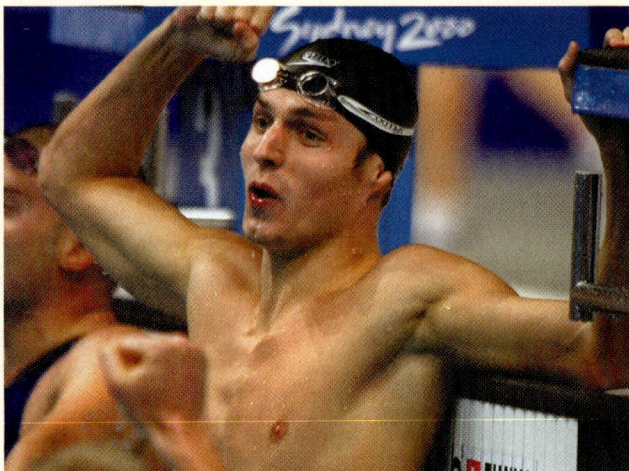

Pieter van den Hoogenband (NED) is victorious in the men's 200-metre freestyle

The **men's 100-metre freestyle**, usually dominated by world record holder Alexander Popov (RUS) and Australia's Michael Klim, also fell under the spell of 'Pieter the Great'. Again, it was a thrashing blanket finish and this time the Dutchman touched ahead of the classical Popov and the extroverted Gary Hall Jr (USA). There were loud cheers for Klim, but he missed a medal by 0.01 seconds.

OLYMPIC FACT

The 50-metre freestyle was out of favour in Olympic competition for 80 years from 1904 to 1988. This may have been caused by a brawl that broke out in 1904 after a dead heat.

Dead heat for USA

The **men's 50-metre freestyle** dash for glory was once Popov's domain, but the man he beat in Atlanta, Gary Hall Jr, had his revenge in Sydney. Hall shared gold with countryman Anthony Ervin (USA) in a dead heat. Pieter van den Hoogenband narrowly missed completing a trio of freestyle victories, 0.05 seconds behind for bronze. Popov was an unthinkable sixth, although only a couple of centimetres behind.

Gary Hall Jr (USA) and Anthony Ervin (USA) tie for gold

 See Swimming results on pages 88–90.

Dutch Superstars

With the rivalry between the USA and Australia, and the media focus on the local stars, two Dutch swimmers, Inge de Bruijn and Pieter van den Hoogenband, made a low-key entrance to the Sydney Olympic Games.

Both left adorned with medals, van den Hoogenband with two gold and two bronze and de Bruijn with three gold and a silver. Van den Hoogenband had given notice in Atlanta with a fourth in both the 100-metre and 200-metre freestyle. His great moment came in Sydney when he just beat the home-town hero Ian Thorpe in the 200-metre freestyle. Van den Hoogenband won his second gold medal in the 100-metre freestyle, and broke Michael Klim's short-lived world record, by clocking 47.84 seconds in a semifinal. A favourite with the crowd, van den Hoogenband won hearts with his sportsmanship and friendly personality.

Pieter van den Hoogenband (NED) collected two gold and two bronze in Sydney

Inge de Bruijn (NED) scooped the pool, taking three gold and one silver

Inge de Bruijn's story was different. She was dropped from the Dutch team for Atlanta because of her poor form and attitude, but appeared in the lead-up to Sydney with a string of world records in the freestyle and butterfly. Her sudden emergence caused speculation about banned substances, but she put her form down to a radical training regime, emphatically denying any allegations. In the pool, she was a glamorous figure in a class of her own. She won the 100-metre butterfly in 56.61 seconds, breaking her own world record. In the 100-metre freestyle she again set a world record of 53.77 seconds. To top it off, she won the 50-metre freestyle in 24.32 seconds. De Bruijn's total domination of the pool was awesome.

See Swimming results on pages 88–90.

Inge the superfish

Inge de Bruijn (NED), all lean muscle and glamorous in waterproof make-up and painted nails, was ready for battle as she swam to three individual gold medals. De Bruijn broke her own world record in the **women's 100-metre butterfly**, beating Martina Moravcova (SVK) and veteran Dara Torres (USA). Australia's Petria Thomas was fourth after qualifying second fastest; Susie O'Neill (AUS) was seventh. In the **women's 100-metre freestyle**, de Bruijn established her supremacy early on and maintained it, despite a valiant effort by Therese Alshammar (SWE), who had to settle for silver. Dara Torres and Jenny Thompson, two great American campaigners, shared the bronze medal. Again, in the **women's 50-metre freestyle** it was de Bruijn, Alshammar, then Torres.

Inge de Bruijn (NED), one of the most successful swimmers in the competition

Eric the eel

You could have watched the start of this **men's 100-metre freestyle** heat, gone out for a cuppa and come back to see the finish. For a time, however, it seemed there would not be a finish as Eric Moussambani of Equatorial Guinea, thrashed ever so slowly towards the wall. Without the roars of encouragement from the crowd, Moussambani may not have made it. He finished and won (his two opponents were disqualified) in a time of 1:52.72. Countries are free to enter any athlete they decide is worthy, and Eric fitted the bill. Just to see his ear-to-ear grin, on managing to complete the swim, was worth it.

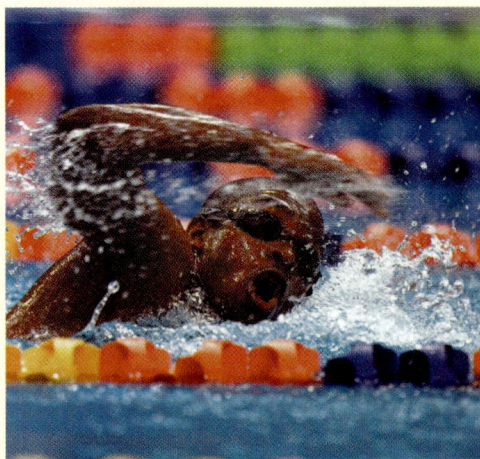

Solo swimmer Eric Moussambani (GEQ) focuses on completing his heat in the men's 100-metre freestyle

 See Swimming results on pages 88–90.

King Krayzelburg in his domain

The Olympic Games was a stage for some of the world's most dominant sporting personalities, and Lenny Krayzelburg (USA) was up there with the best of them. The master of backstroke, Krayzelburg had the physique, good looks and cool style to match. No other competitor could come near 'Lennyland' as he powered to gold in the **men's 200-metre backstroke**. Behind him finished 15-year-old, and heir apparent, Aaron Peirsol (USA), and a fraction later in third place was Matt Welsh (AUS). Welsh then completed an impressive double when he took silver behind Krayzelburg in the **men's 100-metre backstroke**. 'He [Matt] gave me a run for this gold medal,' said Krayzelburg. 'I thought it would take a world record to win.' As it happened, it took an Olympic record of 53.72 seconds.

Lenny Krayzelburg (USA), top of the class in the men's 200-metre backstroke

Matt Welsh (AUS), off to a flying start in the men's 100-metre backstroke

Romania's golden light

Sixteen-year-old Diana Mocanu (ROM) obtained her country's first-ever gold medal in swimming when she stormed through the last few metres of the **women's 100-metre backstroke**. She edged out world No.1 Mai Nakamura (JPN), posting an Olympic record of 1:00.21 along the way. With a second gold, this time in the **women's 200-metre backstroke**, Mocanu confirmed the promise of more great things to come at future Olympic Games.

Diana Mocanu (ROM) takes home Romania's first-ever gold medal in swimming

See Swimming results on pages 88–90.

Madame Freestyle

Susie O'Neill (AUS) thrilled a capacity crowd at the Sydney International Aquatic Centre with a stunning win in the **women's 200-metre freestyle**. It was one of O'Neill's toughest races, but the adoring crowd was right behind her. O'Neill was in front at the 100-metre mark and went on to hold off determined finishes by Martina Moravcova (SVK) and Claudia Poll (CRC) who came second and third. She turned from the wall with that familiar wide-eyed look and was then assailed by a deafening roar as the crowd rose to applaud her. 'Madame Butterfly' had just been crowned 'Madame Freestyle'.

The American express

A bubbly American by the name of Misty Hyman rained on Australia's parade in the **women's 200-metre butterfly**.

Just as Susie O'Neill was poised to claim another victory for Australia, the 21-year-old American stole the show. Hyman was leading at the halfway mark and refused to be hauled in by either O'Neill or her adversary Petria Thomas (AUS). Hyman hit the wall and went into overdrive, in a genuine display of joy and disbelief. O'Neill was gracious in defeat as she and Petria Thomas mounted the podium to receive silver and bronze respectively.

Susie O'Neill (AUS) opens her Sydney campaign with a win in the women's 200-metre freestyle

OLYMPIC FACT

Kevin Berry swam a world record time of 2:06.6 to win gold at the 1964 Olympic Games. Susie O'Neill swam the same time 34 years later to win Commonwealth gold in Kuala Lumpur.

An excited Misty Hyman (USA) claims victory in the women's 200-metre butterfly

See Swimming results on pages 88–90.

Susie O'Neill
Golden girl

Star swimmer, Susie O'Neill (AUS)

For someone who had an early fear of water, Susie O'Neill has spent a magnificent decade at the top of her sport.

As she climbed from the pool at the end of a gruelling Sydney Olympic Games campaign, O'Neill could boast medals won at every international meet she has contested since the 1990 Commonwealth Games.

Born in Mackay on 2 August 1973, O'Neill received her first coaching at the age of 8, and at 14 began swimming butterfly. It was to become her favourite event. Her first Olympic medal came in Barcelona in 1992, when she won bronze in the 200-metre butterfly. Four years later, she won gold in the same event. In Sydney, O'Neill had to settle for silver, but 24 hours earlier, she'd made sure her Olympic career would end on a golden note, by winning the 200-metre freestyle.

Earlier in her career, O'Neill had acquired the nickname Madame Butterfly, a name originally given to American swimmer Mary T. Meagher. Meagher's name had been in the record books since 1982 as the world record holder for the 200-metre butterfly when O'Neill lined up at the Australian Olympic Selection Trials in May. Two minutes and 5.81 seconds later, the oldest world record in swimming was broken, and O'Neill had achieved her ambition to own that time herself.

O'Neill is notoriously shy, and persuading her to talk about her career and achievements is never easy. Others, however, have recognised her contribution. She was Australian Swimmer of the Year in 1995; Female Olympian of the Year in 1996; and Australian Female Athlete of the Year in 1998. She has also been awarded the Order of Australia. At the end of the Sydney 2000 Olympic Games she was one of eight athletes to be inducted into the International Olympic Committee. It seems O'Neill's contribution to world sport isn't over yet.

See Swimming results on pages 88–90.

Froelander in front

Michael Klim and his Australian team-mate Geoff Huegill were expected to fight out the **men's 100-metre butterfly**; the anticipated result was Klim first and Huegill second. But Lars Froelander (SWE) hadn't read the script. He powered through the last 20 metres to edge Klim out by 0.18 of a second, with Huegill in third place. Klim, the current world record holder, and Huegill, had both swum faster times than Froelander in the lead-up races, but the gold medal night belonged to the Swede.

Australia's hero in the **men's 200-metre butterfly** was 20-year-old Justin Norris from Newcastle. He grabbed bronze behind the world record holder Tom Malchow (USA), and Denys Sylant'yev (UKR). Norris later said of his race: 'I don't think I would have done it swimming with my head. I swam with my heart'.

Lars Froelander (SWE) takes gold, while Michael Klim (AUS) and Geoff Huegill (AUS) claim silver and bronze

A radiant Justin Norris (AUS) takes bronze in the men's 200-metre butterfly

Dolan's triumph

Tom Dolan (USA) was the emphatic winner of the **men's 400-metre individual medley** – he raised his arms, smashed the water, hooted and hollered in true American style. Dolan had just lowered his 6-year-old world record by 0.54 seconds. Erik Vendt (USA) took silver and Curtis Myden (CAN) bronze. Dolan had to be content with silver in the **men's 200-metre individual medley** after he lost the race to the exuberant Massimiliano Rosolino (ITA). Tom Wilkens (USA) was third.

Tom Dolan (USA) confirms his supremacy in the men's 400-metre individual medley

Yana Klochkova (UKR) dominated the women's 200-metre and 400-metre medleys

Big plans afoot

It was a sign of things to come. Yana Klochkova (UKR) broke the **women's 400-metre individual medley** world record by 1.20 seconds, in a time of 4:33.59. Only 18 years of age, Klochkova is already to the future: 'I have some big plans and many of them', she said. This proved no idle boast when four days later she also won the **women's 200-metre individual medley**, in an Olympic record time of 2:10.68.

Old foes meet again

Susie O'Neill (AUS) and her Australian 'angels' Petria Thomas, Giaan Rooney and Kirsten Thomson, faced a mighty United States team led by Jenny Thompson in the **women's 4 x 200-metre freestyle relay**. The Australians gave everything they had but could not peg back the narrow lead. Their silver medal swim of 7:58.52 was an Australian record, only 0.72 seconds behind the USA. Again, in the **women's 4 x 100-metre freestyle relay**, it was the American powerhouse of Amy van Dyken, Dara Torres, Courtney Shealy and Jenny Thompson that dominated. The Americans broke China's world record, clocking 3:36.61.

HIGHLIGHT

Two Americans in the women's 4 x 100-metre freestyle relay were dubbed 'the swimming grandmas'. Dara Torres, 33, has been to four Olympic Games, and Jenny Thompson, 27, has seven gold medals from three Olympic Games.

The women's 4 x 100-metre freestyle relay team (USA), cheer Jenny Thompson as she brings home the gold

See Swimming results on pages 88–90.

The dream machine

Australia and the USA faced off in one of the most highly charged events of the Sydney Olympic Games, thanks to the comments of Gary Hall Jr (USA) that his team would 'smash the Australians like guitars'. The moment of truth was the **men's 4 x 100-metre freestyle relay**. Michael Klim (AUS) led out in a record-breaking first swim followed by Chris Fydler (AUS) and Ashley Callus (AUS) who showed their class as they maintained the lead. And then came the amazing last leg, with Ian Thorpe (AUS) cruising past the whirlwind Hall. Thorpe touched first, was hauled from the pool by his ecstatic team-mates, and the crowd roared as the four played air guitar on the pool deck. The Australians then rubbed salt in the wound in the **men's 4 x 200-metre freestyle relay**, with Klim and Thorpe leading fellow Australians Todd Pearson and William Kirby in an effort that took them over 5 seconds clear of their rivals. The Americans had to settle for silver.

Michael Klim (AUS) and his teammates play to a full house after snatching victory in the men's 4 x 100-metre freestyle relay

Revenge in the medleys

In the **women's 4 x 100-metre team medley**, Jenny Thompson and Dara Torres led B. J. Bedford and Megan Quann (USA) to a world record of 3:58.30, smashing the previous world best of 4:01.67. The Australian silver medallists – Dyana Calub, Leisel Jones, Petria Thomas and Susie O'Neill – were also inside the old world record. Not to be outdone in the **men's 4 x 100-metre team medley**, the USA took gold in 3:33.73, another world record. Australia's Matt Welsh, Regan Harrison, Geoff Huegill and the ever-present Michael Klim were second with a time of 3:35.27.

A new world record for the USA in the women's 4 x 100-metre team medley

Hackett crowned king

After seven days of exciting swimming competition, the big event for Australia was on the final day – it was the **men's 1500-metre freestyle**. Kieren Perkins (AUS), an Australian legend, had proved he could come back from the wilderness when he snatched an amazing victory in Atlanta in 1996. In Sydney, he swam the fastest heat and declared himself ready for action. But could he do it again?

Grant Hackett (AUS) had been a lost soul all week, unable to find form and without a gold medal performance. He had been dropped from the final **200-metre freestyle relay** team, and there were rumours of illness and breakdown, and endless media speculation.

Hackett showed from the start that he was not going to crumble. This was the big one and he wouldn't miss it for the world. He hit the front early and then pulled away from Perkins. This was front running, reminiscent of Perkins's remarkable swim in Atlanta. But all of Australia was waiting for the legendary comeback from Perkins, for the lead to be whittled down and the leader overcome.

Hackett dug deep, finding the strength and courage to continue; he claimed the gold medal in 14:48.33. It was well outside Perkins's world record time of 14:41.66, but the triumphant fist reaching out of the water told the crowd that a personal burden had been lifted. Perkins took silver and was predictably gracious in defeat. 'You deserve this', were his first words to Hackett, and he later told the press: 'All credit to Grant. He's been up there for four years. I gave it everything I had tonight'.

And with that, one of the giants of Australian swimming departed modestly, handing the mantle of greatness to a new champion.

Grant Hackett (AUS) and Kieren Perkins (AUS) after the race of their lives

OLYMPIC FACT

Grant Hackett was the sixth Australian to win the men's 1500-metre freestyle Olympic gold medal, following Kieren Perkins (1992 and 1996), Bob Windle (1964), John Konrads (1960), Murray Rose (1956) and Boy Charlton (1924).

A triumphant Grant Hackett (AUS) shows he has what it takes to win gold

See Swimming results on pages 88–90.

Synchronized Swimming

Golden double for synchronized star

At the Games, the synchronized swimming had its own brand of intensity and dedicated fans as medals were contested in team and duet swimming. Beneath the flashing smiles, swirling arms and pointed toes, were endless hours of practice, some amazing underwater endurance and wonderful grace and control.

Canada – a continual favourite since the sport was introduced on the Olympic program in 1984 – is now the only team to have scored a medal at every Olympic Games. In Sydney, the Canadians took bronze in the team event, in which eight swimmers represent their country.

Russia dominated the competition in both duet and team swimming, with Maria Kisseleva (RUS) and Olga Brusnikina (RUS) winning gold medals in both events. Kisseleva and her partner Brusnikina scored 99.580 from a possible 100 in the **duet** competition.

In the **team** event the Russians scored several perfect 10s en route to the gold medal. Their final score was 99.146.

Marissa Kisseleva (RUS) and Olga Brusnikina (RUS) take gold in the women's duet event

The team free routine delivered gold to the Russian women's synchronized swimming team

HIGHLIGHT

At the Sydney Olympic Games, there were three sets of twins in synchronized swimming: Livia and Lucia Allarova (SVK), Carolina and Isabela Moraes (BRA); and Heba and Sara Abdel Gawad (EGY).

 See Synchronized Swimming results on page 90.

Water Polo

Heart-stopping victory

Two seconds doesn't sound like much time to do anything. But it was enough to pick up a water polo ball, look for options, pass it down the pool, set up an attack, and then flick it into the net to snatch victory. This was the scene played out at the packed water polo stadium in Ryde where the host nation took gold in the **women's water polo**. The Australian's had relinquished their 3–2 lead to the USA, only 12 seconds before the end of the game, and were left with only a narrow window of time when the game restarted. With scores locked at 3–3, and extra time looming in the event of a draw, Yvette Higgins's (AUS) shot flew into the top corner of the net as the hooter sounded. There was a stunned silence and then roars of sheer delight both in and out of the water. The win was especially sweet for the Australian team who had led the fight to have women's water polo included in the Olympic program.

The victorious women's water polo team (AUS)

Hungary grabs gold

The powerful European teams dominated the **men's water polo**, with Hungary winning the gold medal, its seventh in total, but the first since Montreal in 1976. Hungary beat Russia 13–6, with Tibor Benedek (HUN) scoring four goals. Yugoslavia beat Atlanta gold medallist Spain 8–3 to take the bronze.

HIGHLIGHT

Spanish water polo captain Manuel Estiarte was representing his country for the sixth time at the Sydney Olympic Games, having first played in Moscow in 1980.

See Water Polo results on page 90. **21**

Archery

Fairweather's golden arrow

Few Australians would have imagined an archer would become the nation's seventh gold medallist of the Sydney Olympics Games, but Simon Fairweather (AUS) achieved that unique distinction on a blustery afternoon at Homebush Bay. In an amazing display of marksmanship, Fairweather secured Australia's first Olympic medal in archery in front of a jubilant crowd.

Simon Fairweather (AUS) shoots for gold

Fairweather, named Young Australian of the Year in 1991 and 1992, found himself in the **men's individual** final against Victor Wunderle of the USA. He was overcome with emotion when he won gold. Victor Wunderle (USA) won silver and Wietse van Alten (NED) took bronze.

Target – Sydney 2000

Korea dominated the **women's individual** competition, making a clean sweep of the medal pool. Yun Mi-Jin won gold, from Kim Nam-Soon. Kim Soo-Nyung took the bronze. In the **team** competition, Korea won gold in both events. The Korean men were too strong, taking gold ahead of Italy and the USA, while the Korean women defeated the Ukraine in the gold medal round. Germany won the bronze.

A clean sweep for Koreans Yun Mi-Jin, Kim Nam-Soon and Kim Soo-Nyung

Athletics

Track

The fastest man on earth

He walks the walk, talks the talk, and in Sydney, he flew down the track to win the blue-ribbon event of athletics, the **men's 100 metres**. Maurice Greene (USA) or 'MO' for short, finished in a time of 9.87 seconds, just edging out his roommate and training partner Ato Boldon (TRI). Greene had looked focused and aggressive in the heats and semifinals, but mouthed a 'Thank you, God' to the sky as he crossed the line in the final. 'I was trying not to cry, I was overwhelmed with excitement and everything' said a pumped up Greene. 'It is really hard to work for four years for something that only lasts nine seconds'. One of the shoes that had carried him into Olympic history was then thrown into the stands!

One casualty along the way was Matt Shirvington (AUS), who narrowly missed out on the final.

Maurice Greene (USA) claims victory in the men's 100 metres

In a class of her own

The result of the **women's 100 metres** was a foregone conclusion. From the moment Marion Jones (USA) stared down the track and then lowered her head, waiting for the starter's gun, it was the Jones show. She smashed the opposition, finishing in 10.75 seconds, at least 5 metres ahead of her nearest opponent Ekaterini Thanou (GRE). Tanya Lawrence (JAM) was third, 0.01 seconds ahead of the veteran and crowd favourite Merlene Ottey (JAM). Again, the **women's 200 metres** was all Jones. The two Australians, Melinda Gainsford-Taylor, and Cathy Freeman, finished sixth and seventh respectively. Both had run their fastest 200s for the year. That still wasn't enough to touch the Jones juggernaut.

Marion Jones (USA) on her way to gold in the women's 100 metres

See Athletics results on pages 91–2.

Marion Jones
Just awesome!

Marion Jones's (USA) mission in Sydney was five gold medals. As the days progressed, and Marion scorched the field in both the 100 and 200 metres, it seemed her ambition would be fulfilled.

Born in Los Angeles, California, in 1975, Jones was to become a terrific basketball player. She was named California Division 1 Player of the Year and helped North Carolina to the NCAA title in her first year of college basketball. It was here that she met C. J. Hunter who was the university's throw coach. He prompted her to return to track and field.

The Los Angeles Olympic Games of 1984 had made a deep impression on Jones. After watching the pre-Games parade, she wrote on her bedroom blackboard: I will be an Olympic champion in 1992. However, this was not to be and she had to wait until Sydney to fulfil her ambition.

The chances are she will now concentrate her sights on the Athens Olympic Games. As proven, she has a virtual mortgage on the premier sprint events, and could easily gather strong relay teams around her next time, and work hard at her long jump. She has the physique but not the technique for the last event, landing two footed and upright like the jumpers of old.

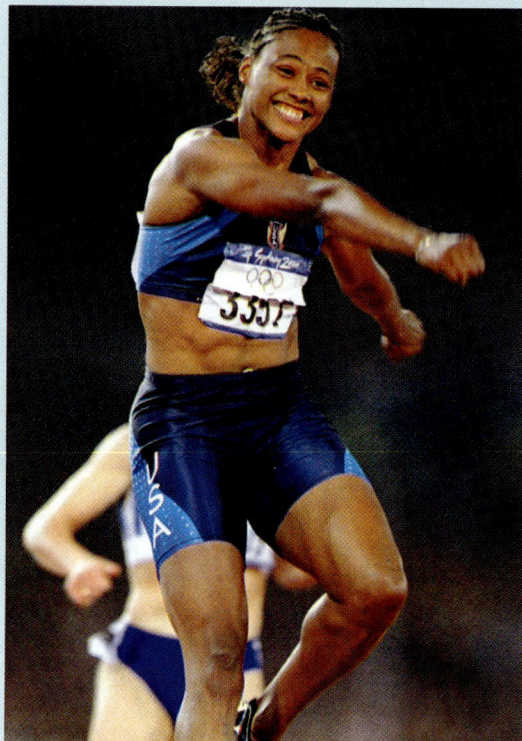

Marion Jones (USA), one of the most impressive athletes of our time

Jones had other demons to conquer at the Sydney Olympic Games, as her husband, the gigantic shot putter C. J. Hunter, was revealed to have tested positive to nandrolone. She refused to be drawn into the matter, other than to say that she supported her husband's denials.

On the track she displays a variety of demeanours, including youthful and smiling when being introduced or after a race, or intent and serious when she gets down to the business in hand. She is the first Olympic athlete to take the sprint double in twelve years, and this record has elevated her into the class of her great compatriots Jesse Owens, Carl Lewis and Florence Griffith-Joyner. Still, Marion Jones's race is far from over.

See Athletics results on pages 91–2.

Kon the Greek

Konstantinos Kenteris (GRE) was the only white man in the final of the **men's 200 metres**, starkly contrasted against the seven impressive black athletes who surrounded him on the blocks. The event was supposed to be a contest between the 200 metres world champion Maurice Greene (USA) and world record holder Michael Johnson (USA). In their absence, Ato Boldon (TRI) was the favourite. Kenteris surged down the straight to win, and became the first Greek to take a gold medal in athletics since Spyridon Louis won the first marathon in 1896. Darren Campbell (GBR) was second and Ato Boldon (TRI) third.

Konstantinos Kenteris (GRE), the first Greek to take a gold medal in athletics since 1896

Twenty-four carat gold

The crowd was still emotionally charged from Cathy Freeman's win when the big man of track athletics hit the blocks for the **men's 400 metres**. Michael Johnson (USA) looked a winner and had the record to prove it, including double gold in the Atlanta Games and world records for both the 200 and 400 metres. With his strange, upright running style and fearful pace he was soon in the clear, leaving the others behind. He careered to the line in 43.84 seconds, well ahead of team-mate Alvin Harrison (USA) who was followed by Gregory Haughton (JAM). Johnson's much talked about 24 carat gold shoes had carried him to another win.

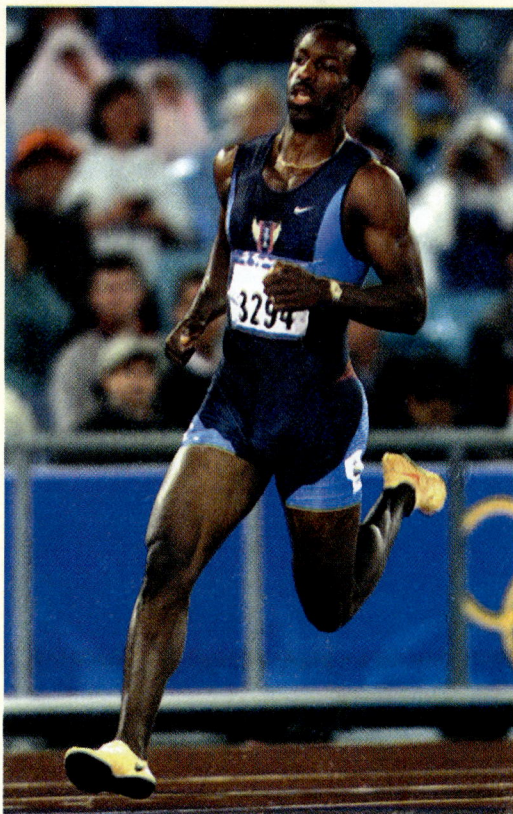

Michael Johnson's (USA) golden shoes carry him to victory in the men's 400 metres

See Athletics results on pages 91–2.

The race that united a nation

The people of Australia had been waiting for this moment for at least four years. Cathy Freeman (AUS) had blitzed her opponents in the heats of the **women's 400 metres**, but this was the final. She walked onto the track, dressed for business, in the all-in-one running suit. Then the race was on, amid tumultuous noise. Freeman made little impact on the field initially, and Lorraine Graham (JAM) and Katharine Merry (GBR) looked threatening. They reached the final bend with Freeman third. Suddenly she accelerated, pulling away to win easily in the end. Afterwards she just slumped on the track. A huge burden had been lifted. Then the celebrations began.

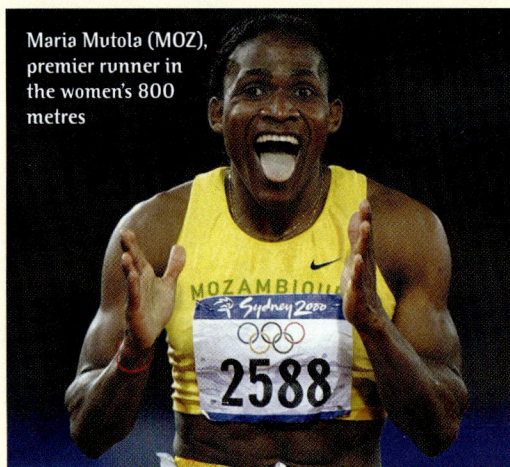

Maria Mutola (MOZ), premier runner in the women's 800 metres

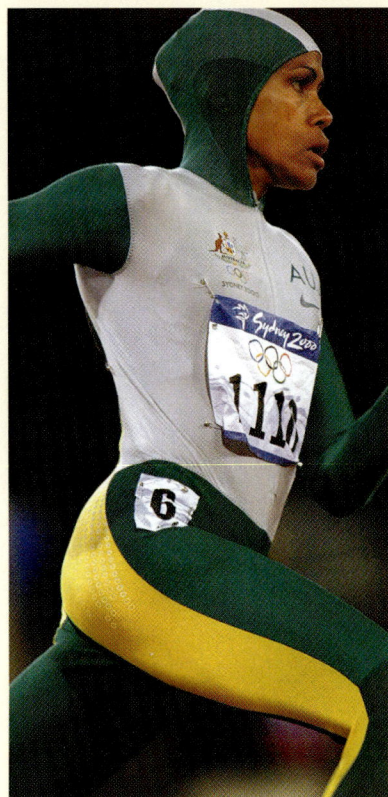

Cathy Freeman (AUS) carries the hopes of Australians in the women's 400 metres

Mutola magic and more

The **women's 800 metres** was a breakthrough for the immensely strong Maria Mutola (MOZ). She had been a premier runner in the event for a decade, but her only Olympic medal to date had been a bronze at the Atlanta Games. This time she ran from the front, was passed in the last lap, but kicked out early for a long, strong finish. Behind her Stephanie Graf (AUT) ran second and Kelly Holmes (GBR) third.

In the **men's 800 metres**, Nils Schumann (GER) was the surprise package. He avoided all the bumping and interference in the second lap and kicked out to lead the rest of the field until the finish. Wilson Kipketer (DEN), a great 800 runner and the favorite, took silver and Aissa Djabir Said-Guerni (ALG) bronze.

HIGHLIGHT

Maria Mutola holds national records in Mozambique for every distance from 200 metres to 3000 metres. A national holiday was declared in Mozambique on the news of her 800 metres win.

Cathy Freeman
Woman of destiny

Somehow Cathy Freeman (AUS) has become more than an elite athlete. Her Aboriginal pride, rare mixture of girlishness and serious intent, and her long run of achievements set against injury and personal difficulty, have captured the heart of the nation.

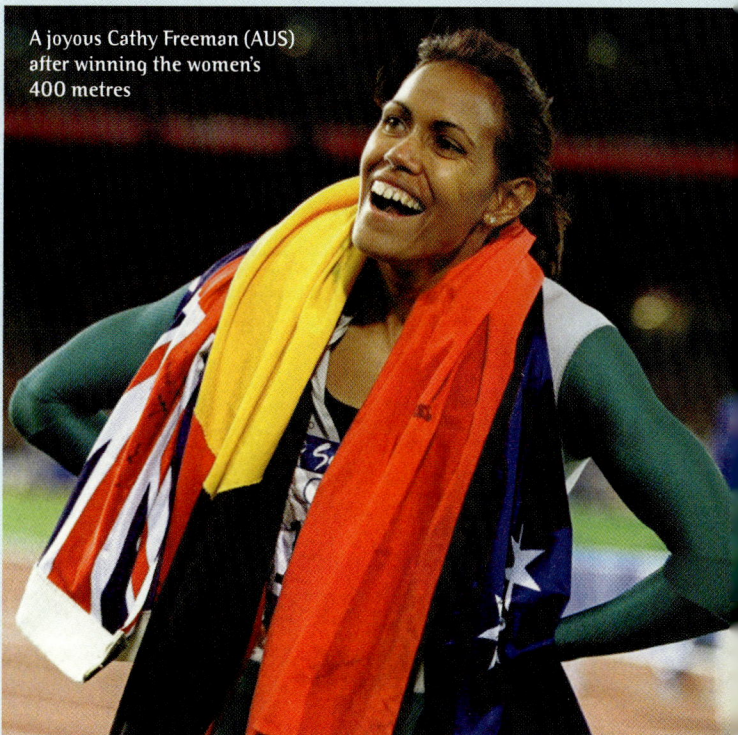

A joyous Cathy Freeman (AUS) after winning the women's 400 metres

Public interest began long ago when Freeman carried the Aboriginal and Australian flags at the Commonwealth Games in Victoria, Canada, to the outrage of some officials. Interest grew even more when she ran a gallant second, at the Atlanta Olympic Games, to the great star of the 400 metres, Marie-Jose Perec. Perec's long-standing cat-and-mouse game with Cathy continued this year, and the French star failed to keep the ultimate appointment when she fled from Sydney before the big race.

With questions of reconciliation and the renewal of a proud Aboriginal identity on Australia's political and social agenda, the slim figure of Cathy Freeman took on added symbolism. The fast running girl from Mackay, the student from Melbourne, the globe-trotting athlete and media drawcard was being held up as the modern symbol of Australian identity.

The stage was set when Freeman was given the honour of lighting the cauldron at Stadium Australia, a task that may have put even more pressure on her to win gold in her event. Her victory in the 400-metres left her slumped, amazed at the enormity of it all. And then she greeted her family, grabbed the Australian and Aboriginal flags and ran out to meet the people. It was a unifying moment in the history of Australia.

See Athletics results on pages 91–2.

Irina the great

The **women's 400-metre hurdles** was a fairy story for Irina Privalova (RUS), the former champion sprinter who switched to hurdles after a spate of injuries. The 31-year-old made her hurdle debut in January 2000, when reportedly her form sent shudders through her rivals. She beat Deon Hemmings (JAM) and Nouzha Bidouane (MAR).

Olga Shishigina (KAZ) won the **women's 100-metre hurdles**, with Glory Alozie (NGR) second and Melissa Morrison (USA) third, after champion Gail Devers (USA) crashed out in the semi-final with a torn hamstring.

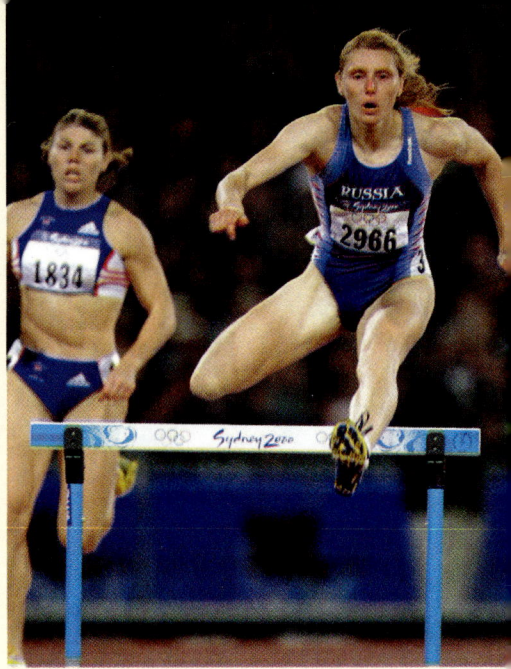

Irina Privalova (RUS), champion sprinter turned hurdler

Double eludes Szabo

Gabriela Szabo (ROM) only produces little steps, but this experienced runner can last the distance. In the **women's 5000 metres** she stayed in or near the front, riding the surges and then slowing down the pace at the front. In the end she just flew away from a gallant Sonia O'Sullivan (IRL) and Gete Wami (ETH), to claim the gold.

Not so easy, however, was the **women's 1500 metres**, which lived up to its reputation as a notoriously rough race. Szabo was seeking an historic 1500–5000 double, but had to hurdle a fallen runner at the 800-metre mark and lost 10 to 15 metres. Even so she made a blistering run for bronze behind Nouria Merah-Benida (ALG), who took gold, and Violeta Szekely (ROM), who took silver, and had managed to avoid all the trouble.

HIGHLIGHT

Sixteen-year-old Georgie Clarke (AUS) made the semifinal of the women's 1500 metres. She stayed with the field, tracking them with an easy, long stride; a promise of great things to come.

The Romanian flag flies high after Gabriela Szabo's (ROM) win in the women's 5000 metres

See Athletics results on pages 91–2.

Disaster strikes Saville

Jane Saville (AUS) was only 120 metres from a gold medal in the **women's 20-kilometre walk** when disaster struck. In the tunnel en route to the stadium she was assailed by the chief judge Lamberto Vacchi. He was holding up a red card and told her that she had been disqualified for lifting (losing contact with the ground). She had received two warnings during the race, but was streets ahead and thought she was moving easily and within the rules. A stunned crowd watched as Saville burst into tears. She later won praise for her dignified handling of the situation. The winner Wang Liping (CHN) received a polite but muted reception as she entered the stadium.

A disappointed Jane Saville (AUS) after her disqualification in the women's 20-kilometre walk

Walking for gold

Robert Korzeniowski (POL) won the **men's 20-kilometre walk** in the first track event of the Sydney Olympic Games. He confirmed his greatness in the **men's 50-kilometre walk** when he became the first man to win both titles. He also scored back-to-back wins, following up his 50-kilometre success at the Atlanta Games. Korzeniowski's win in the 20-kilometre walk was an Olympic best time, but he was confirmed the winner only after the disqualification of the first man across the line, Bernardo Segura (MEX).

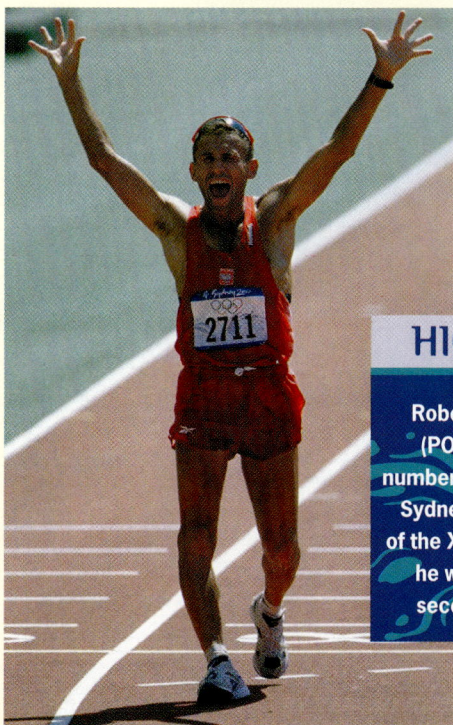

Robert Korzeniowski (POL), the first man to win both the 20- and 50-kilometre walks

HIGHLIGHT

Robert Korzeniowski (POL) said his race number '2711' was lucky – Sydney was the Games of the XXVII Olympiad and he was going for his second gold medal.

African Legends

For many years now, the world's most gifted and determined long-distance runners have come from East Africa. But what makes them so special?

Millon Wolde (ETH) wins the men's 5000 metres

Noah Ngeny (KEN) claims gold in the men's 1500 metres

Since the emergence of Abebe Bikila (ETH), running has never quite been the same. Many remember his victory in the Olympic marathon in 1960, when he ran barefoot through the streets of Rome. He repeated the feat in Tokyo in 1964. This time he wore shoes. Mamo Wolde (ETH) then completed a hat-trick of Ethiopian marathon wins when he took gold in Mexico City in 1968. Miruts Yifter (ETH), dubbed 'Yifter the Shifter', was another legend who won two gold medals in Moscow for the 5000 and the 10 000 metres. And so it goes on, a roll-call of honour listing some of the most impressive athletes of our times whose gift for running seems god-given.

In Sydney we saw Haile Gebrselassie (ETH), master of the 10 000 metres and Assefa Mezgebu (ETH) who took bronze in the same event; Millon Wolde (ETH) who won the 5000 metres, and of course Gezahgne Abera (ETH) and Tesfaye Tola (ETH) who took gold and bronze in the marathon. The Ethiopian women have also had their fair share of success with Gete Wami and Derartu Tulu grabbing the limelight in Sydney.

Neighbouring Kenya has also produced its fair share of super runners. The legend, Kip Keino, who, against his doctor's advice, jumped a bus to get to the stadium for the start of the 1500 metres final in 1968. There was a traffic jam, so he jogged the last 3 kilometres to the stadium and went on to win the final.

In Sydney we saw Paul Tergat (KEN), another distance runner who to date has always been just a step behind Gebrselassie; Reuben Kosgei (KEN) winner of the 3000-metre steeplechase, and Wilson Boit Kipketer (KEN), silver medallist in the same event; Eric Wainaina (KEN) who took silver in the marathon and Noah Ngeny (KEN) and Bernard Lagat (KEN) who took gold and bronze in the 1500 metres.

So, what is it that makes them tick? Various theories have been put forward including high-altitude training, genetics, a strict training regime and the like. But ultimately it is their determination to be up there with the best in the world that makes them succeed.

See Athletics results on pages 91–2.

Haile the master

It was a race to savour in the **men's 10 000 metres** – Haile Gebrselassie (ETH) and Paul Tergat (KEN) head-to-head for Olympic gold. Tergat tried to break the Ethiopian who had beaten him in the Atlanta Games, but as he began his finishing sprint, he was boxed in by Assefa Mezgebu (ETH). Gebrselassie, in a flat sprint, then pipped Tergat for the gold medal by 0.09 seconds. In the **men's 5000 metres**, Millon Wolde (ETH), showed

A smiling Haile Gebrselassie (ETH) crosses the line at the end of the men's 10 000 metres

himself a worthy successor to the master when he beat Ali Saidi-Sief (ALG) and world No. 1 Brahim Lahlafi (MAR). Wolde charged to the front, producing a blistering last lap of 54 seconds. Derartu Tulu (ETH) became the first woman to win distance events at two separate Olympic Games when she beat Gete Wami (ETH) during a magnificent **women's 10 000 metres**. Tulu won by a handsome margin following up on her great win at the Barcelona Olympics.

Tragedy for El Guerrouj

The **men's 1500 metres** final was again dominated by the Africans but this time it was not quite a fairytale ending. At least not for the favourite Hicham El Guerrouj (MAR) who had waited four long years to exorcise the demons of Atlanta. In 1996, with only one lap to go, the Moroccan had been ready to shoot to the front when disaster struck. He bumped into Noureddine Morceli (ALG), fell, staggered back into the race, but finished last. In Sydney, El Guerrouj was beaten again, this time by a desperate surge from Noah Ngeny (KEN) in the last 15 metres. A shattered El Guerrouj sank to the track in disbelief and could only contemplate what might have been. For the gifted middle-distance runner, unbeaten since 1997, silver was of little consolation.

A shattered Hicham El Guerrouj (MAR) after missing out on the gold medal in the men's 1500 metres

See Athletics results on pages 91–2.

Bahamas takes gold

The USA was bidding for its sixth consecutive gold medal in the **women's 4 x 100-metre relay**, but had to lower its colours to the quality line-up from the Bahamas. Jamaica was second, giving Merlene Ottey her eighth Olympic medal at the age of 40. The Americans had to settle for bronze. Unfortunately, Australia went no further than a dropped baton in round one.

After the aberration in the first relay, the USA was back in charge in the **women's 4 x 400-metre relay**. Marion Jones (USA) powered through the fourth leg, collecting her third gold medal for the Games. Jamaica took silver and the Russian Federation came in for bronze. Australia, with Cathy Freeman and Melinda Gainsford-Taylor in the team, ran a new national record of 3:23.81, but missed out on a medal.

The women's 4 x 100-metre relay team from Bahamas celebrates a golden run

Stars and stripes in charge

The USA has won the **men's 4 x 100-metre relay** fifteen times; ten of those have been in world record time. Therefore it was no surprise when they won in Sydney, this time over Brazil and Cuba. Clearly delighted with their win, the Americans stayed on the track for a while after the race, basking in their glory.

The **men's 4 x 400 metre relay** was another United States powerhouse affair, with Antonio Pettigrew, the Harrison twins, Calvin and Alvin, and Michael Johnson beating Nigeria and Jamaica.

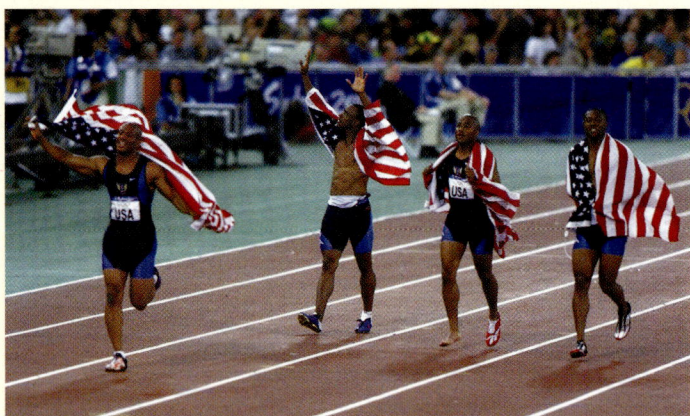

The Americans acknowledge the crowd after winning the men's 4 x 100-metre relay

Michael Johnson
King of the track

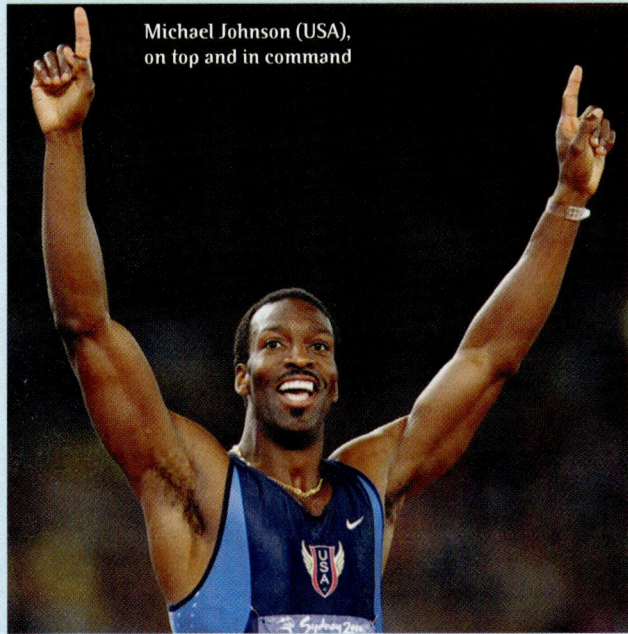

Michael Johnson (USA), on top and in command

Michael Johnson (USA) has left the stage of the Olympics as impressively as he has occupied it through the 1990s – on top and in command. 'This being my last Games, I didn't want to mess it up. I came in winning and I left winning.' He certainly has the statistics to prove it.

In him there is a determination as he walks onto the track, a calmness as he settles into the blocks and an apparently effortless means of propulsion. His piston-engine style of running 'like a man sitting down' had won many college meetings and national championships in early years, but it was on the global stage of the Olympic Games that the world was able to watch and marvel at his speed.

Johnson started his Olympic career at the Barcelona Olympic Games in 1992, was struck down by food poisoning, but was part of the winning relay team. The Atlanta Olympic Games was his time of glory. There he created a world record for the 200 metres in 19.32 seconds, as well as dominating the 400 metres. After the 400 he threw his golden shoes into the crowd, forgetting they had spikes on them!

At 33 years of age, Johnson is still at the top. He is an extremely wealthy man through a host of endorsements and the sponsorship of Nike. As a graduate in marketing, it wouldn't take much for Johnson to reach new heights in sports management, further contributing his talents to a field he knows and loves best.

But for now, this extraordinary athlete nicknamed 'Superman' for obvious reasons, has five gold medals from five events over three Olympic Games. He also has numerous other medals from world championships and other competitions, and they are all the same colour – gold.

See Athletics results on pages 91–2.

Japanese superstar

Naoko Takahashi (JPN) is a household name in Japan. The swarm of Japanese reporters surrounding her training sessions, and every move in Sydney, meant that something special was expected to take place in the **women's marathon**. Takahashi ran the race of a champion, pacing herself perfectly with her tight, economical stride, and staged a thrilling battle with Lidia Simon (ROM) before breaking away to enter the stadium only metres ahead. Takahashi thrilled the crowd with her tough spirit; she won in 2:23:14. It had been a people's race from start to end with spectators lining the route to shout words of encouragement.

Naoko Takahashi (JPN) runs the race of a champion in the women's marathon

African trifecta

The stage of the **men's marathon** across the Harbour Bridge, and through Centennial Park and harbour-side Sydney saw some runners going out hard. But a grittier mood took over through the working-class west and on the way to Homebush. The breakaways and stayers to the end were two Ethiopians Gezahgne Abera and Tesfaye Tola, and Eric Wainaina (KEN). As they raced towards the stadium, Abera caught Wainaina and went on to win by 20 seconds in 2:10:11. A special moment for the Australian crowd came when Steve Moneghetti, running his twenty-second marathon, entered the stadium. He finished tenth, having paced himself through the earlier stages, then winding in the field in true 'Monna' style. The 38-year-old Victorian couldn't have asked for a better end to his career.

HIGHLIGHT

Aquida Amaral of East Timor reached the line in the women's marathon, and bowed down in prayer. Unfortunately, though, it was a lap too soon! She was urged to run on, carried by a wave of applause.

In the men's marathon, Gezahgne Abera (ETH) wins gold, Eric Wainaina (KEN) takes silver and Tesfaye Tola (ETH) secures bronze

Field

Grigorieva jumps for joy

In the **women's pole vault**, talented Tatiana Grigorieva (AUS) had everything to strive for and nothing to lose. Grigorieva, who had come to Australia from the Russian Federation in 1996, gave all for her adopted country whose thunderous support seemed to lift her into the air. The noise of the crowd swelled to a crescendo as she began each run-up and she used this motivation to exceed her competition personal best, jumping 4.55 metres. At this height she was briefly leading Stacy Dragila (USA) and it was a good enough vault for the silver medal. The composed American went one better, leaping to 4.60 metres and securing gold.

A focused Tatiana Grigorieva (AUS) prepares for her run-up in the women's pole vault

Golden vault for USA

There were two fairytale possibilities in the **men's pole vault**. The first was that the great Sergey Bubka (UKR), gold medallist at the Seoul Games, would muster one last effort to shake off the hoodoo that had denied him victory at the Barcelona Games and Atlanta Games. But this was not to be, and he bowed out in the preliminaries. The second was that Viktor Chistiakov (AUS) would win a medal to match that of his wife Tatiana Grigorieva. Chistiakov jumped superbly with a clearance of 5.80 metres, but failed to match the 5.90-metre jumps of the three medal winners Nick Hysong (USA), Lawrence Johnson (USA) and Maksim Tarasov (RUS).

OLYMPIC FACT

There was a sad note in the women's pole vault, when former world record holder Emma George bowed out at the 4.30-metre mark. The popular Australian had not recovered form or confidence since a jumping accident in Germany.

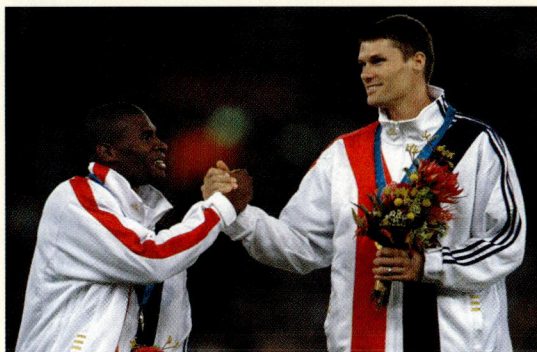

The USA takes gold and silver in the men's pole vault

Russians jump for gold

Javier Sotomayor (CUB), the highest jumper coming into the competition, was brought down by Sergey Kliugin (RUS) as he attempted to emulate his gold medal from Barcelona in the **men's high jump**. Sotomayor led the field when he attacked the bar at 2.32 metres, but there he stayed, watching from under his rain-sodden poncho as Kliugin (RUS) went one

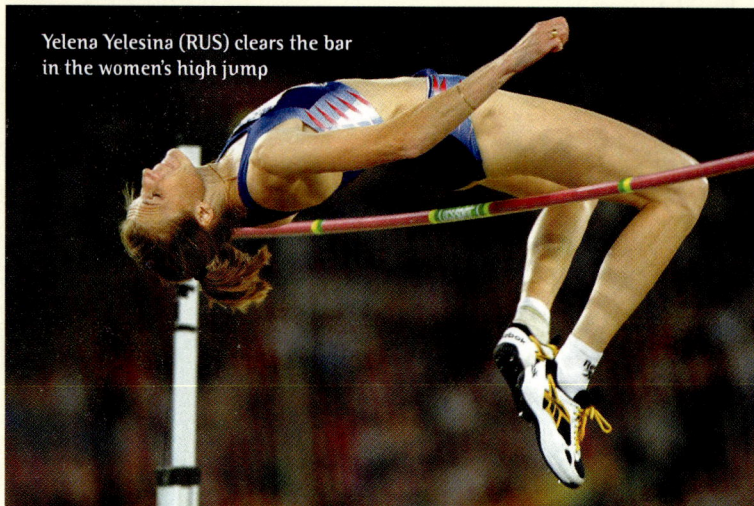

Yelena Yelesina (RUS) clears the bar in the women's high jump

better to 2.35 metres. The **women's high jump** gold went to Yelena Yelesina (RUS) at 2.01 metres.

Victory of the fittest

Australian Louise Currey won silver at the Atlanta Games with a mighty effort in the **women's javelin**. But in Sydney, attempting to throw with an injured knee, she could get no distance and limped away in pain. The final went to Trine Hattestad (NOR), who threw an Olympic record of 68.91 metres. The **men's javelin** created another Olympic superhero in Ján Zelezny (CZE), who became the seventh person, and only the second non-American, to win the same event at three successive Olympic Games. He threw 90.17 metres, an Olympic record.

Edwards takes gold

Jonathan Edwards (GBR) nearly left Sydney when he heard of the death of his mother-in-law, but his wife begged him to stay for the **men's triple jump**. The deeply religious son of an English pastor was rewarded with gold, to back up his silver medal from the Atlanta Games, after jumping 17.71 metres. The **women's triple jump** was dominated by eastern European countries. Tereza Marinova (BUL) won gold with a jump of 15.20 metres.

Ján Zelezny (CZE) has won the men's javelin at three successive Olympic Games

36 See Athletics results on pages 91–2.

Jumping Jai

Jai 'Trigger' Taurima (AUS) with the flowing black hair, lurid sunglasses and necklace does not look like an athlete – until he starts running and jumping. The crowd in the stands was riveted to the **men's long jump** as Taurima jumped further and further up the leader board. Clapping and encouraging the crowd to support him, he took Australian national records at 8.40 and then 8.49 metres. He was leading the competition until old campaigner Ivan Pedroso (CUB) upped the stakes to a mighty 8.55 metres with his final leap. Jumping Jai had a last chance, and the stadium went from a hush to a roar as he started his run-up. He did not make it, but he won the adulation of Australia, and a silver medal as well.

Jai Taurima (AUS), a favourite with the crowd, took silver in the men's long jump

Mighty Marion beaten

The **women's long jump** was on Marion Jones's (USA) agenda in Sydney, but she had to bow to a specialist, Heike Drechsler (GER), who cut the sand for gold at 6.99 metres. The 35-year-old Drechsler had won silver at the Seoul Games, for East Germany, and gold at the Barcelona Games. Drechsler's style was impeccable, while Jones relied on speed to fling herself into the air and hang there as long as possible, before an awkward landing. Jones took bronze behind Drechsler and Fiona May (ITA).

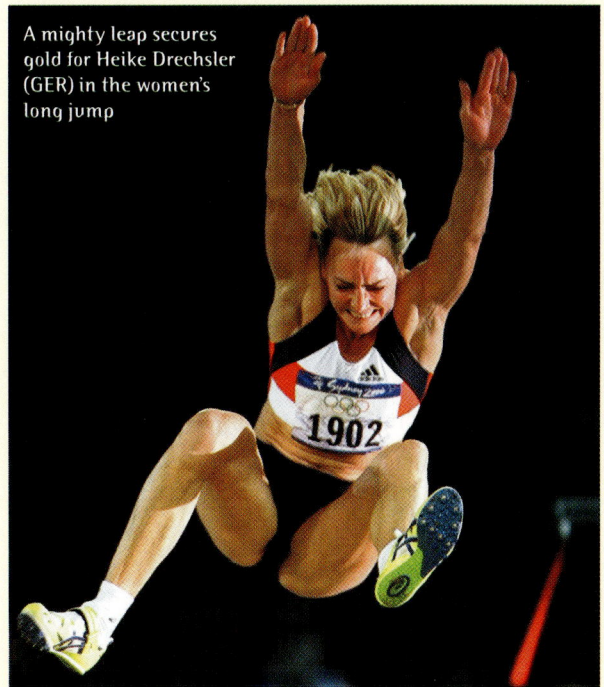

A mighty leap secures gold for Heike Drechsler (GER) in the women's long jump

See Athletics results on pages 91–2.

Spectacular throws

Arsi Harju (FIN) was a surprise winner in a tense fight for the **men's shot put**. The favourites were Adam Nelson (USA) and John Godina (USA), but Harju shaded Nelson by 0.08 metres with a throw of 21.29 metres. The **women's shot put** result was hanging in the balance for most of the long night, but eventually went to Yanina Korolchik (BLR), the only woman to throw past 20 metres.

Arsi Harju (FIN), a surprise winner in the men's shot put

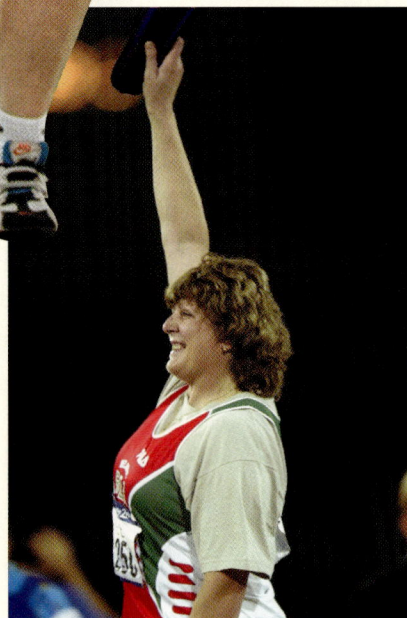

Raining hammers

Hammer throwers prefer sunshine and still air, but on their big night at Stadium Australia, there was driving rain. The gold medal for the **men's hammer throw** was won by Szymon Ziolkowski (POL) with a throw of 80.02 metres. The **women's hammer throw** produced an early thrill when Sydney's Debbie Sosimenko (AUS) started with a Commonwealth record of 67.95 metres. In the end the gold went to 17-year-old Kamila Skolimowska (POL), who threw a new Olympic record of 71.16 metres. Sosimenko finished out of the medals but was all smiles.

Discus winner winds up

Virgilijus Alekna (LTU) had an uncharacteristically poor first throw of 58.55 metres in the first round of the **men's discus**, but he gradually worked up to the form that made him the favourite for the event. In his fifth throw Alekna hit 69.30 metres, enough to give him the gold medal. The **women's discus** was won by the oldest woman in the competition, 39-year-old Ellina Zvereva (BLR).

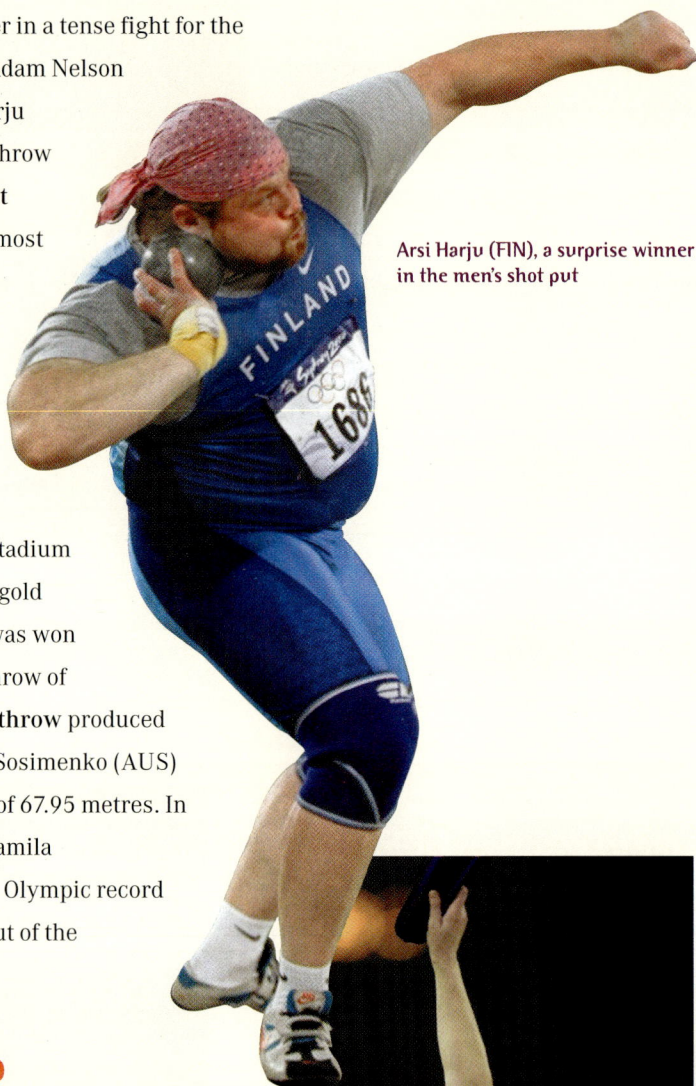

Ellina Zvereva (BLR) wins gold in the women's discus

 See Athletics results on pages 91–2.

Heptathlon leaves Brit dancing

Denise Lewis (GBR) had endured two long days of **heptathlon** competition, and some poor weather on the final day, to win a gold medal with a score of 6584 for the seven events – hurdles, high jump, shot put, 200 metres, long jump, javelin and 800 metres. But she still had the energy to dance around the soggy track, before the gold medal ceremony. The silver medal went to Yelena Prokhorova (RUS) with 6531, with Natalya Sazanovich (BLR) just four points behind. Australia's silver medallist from the Commonwealth Games, Jane Jamieson, was tenth with 6104 points.

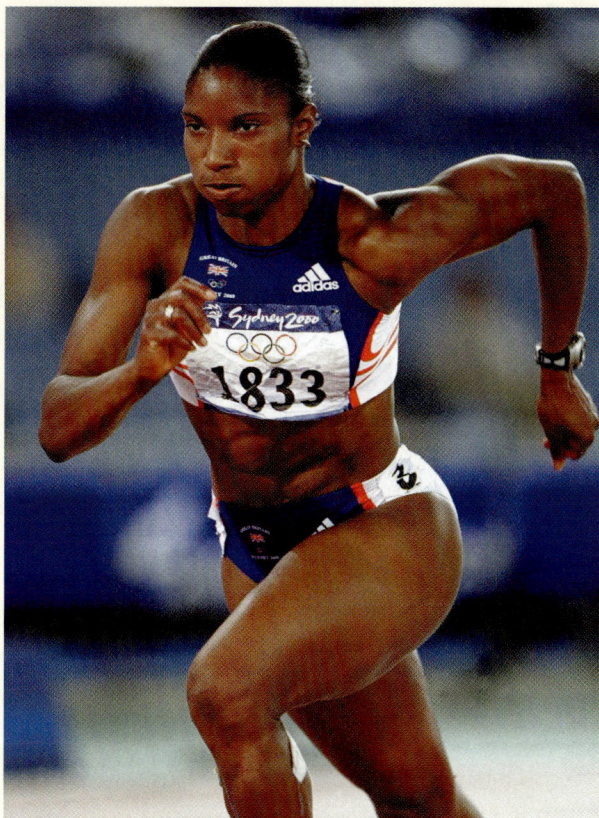

Denise Lewis (GBR), gold medallist in the heptathlon

White flag gives Estonian the decathlon

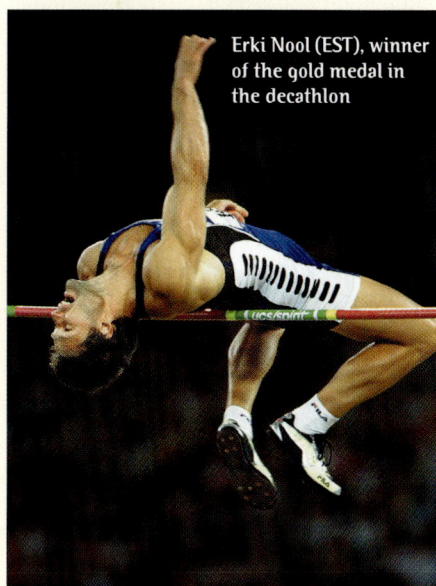

Erki Nool (EST), winner of the gold medal in the decathlon

The gold medal winner of the **decathlon**, Erki Nool (EST), was only allowed to stay in the competition after a referee's white flag in the discus discipline, which overruled a 'no throw' red flag from a judge. Nool had fouled twice, and a third foul would have brought no points in the seventh stage of the ten-event competition. The mark kept Nool in the event, but placed behind American Chris Huffins, who had led for nine events. The final event was the 1500 metres and Nool recorded 4:29.4 to Huffins's 4:38.4 to leapfrog him on the leader board and win the gold medal. Huffins was also passed by Roman Sebrle (CZE), who took silver.

See Athletics results on pages 91–2.

China flies high

China dominated the badminton competition at the Sydney Olympic Games winning four gold, one silver and three bronze medals to comfortably top the medal table. Indonesia was second with one gold and two silver medals. China won the **men's singles** and picked up a bronze in the **women's singles**. It was a clean sweep for China in the **women's doubles** with gold, silver and bronze, and a Chinese combination won the **mixed doubles**. Indonesia took the **men's doubles**, with Korea picking up silver and bronze.

Ge Fei and Gu Jun (CHN) celebrate their win in the women's doubles competition

Ji Xinpeng and Gong Zhichao clinch gold

The result of the **men's singles** final was a major upset. Ji Xinpeng (CHN) had been beaten by Hendrawan (INA) in May 2000 in the prestigious Thomas Cup teams finals, but Ji dominated the opening game at the Sydney 2000 Games. He secured the game with a convincing 15–4 win. Hendrawan fought back bravely, taking a 9–4 lead in the second game, but Ji clinched the win 15–13.

In the **women's singles** final, Camilla Martin (DEN) made history by becoming the first non-Asian player to reach the medal round at the Olympic Games and win a silver, but top seed Gong Zhichao (CHN) won the gold medal with a score of 13–10, 11–3.

Candra Wijaya and Tony Gunawan (INA) on their way to gold in the men's doubles competition

OLYMPIC FACT

Mixed doubles was added to the program in Atlanta in 1996, making badminton the only Olympic sport to feature mixed doubles.

The USA played Cuba in the baseball final

Battle of the heavyweights

The Cubans could hardly believe it – they had lost the **baseball** final. The score? 4–0. It mattered little that the winners were the USA, the country that invented the game. The Cubans left the field stunned. They had won the Olympic baseball competitions at the Barcelona Games and Atlanta Games, and had not lost a world championship since 1939.

The Cuban players opted to leave the post-match press conference without a word, and their manager, Servio Borges, had to be brought back to speak. He said he could not ever remember Cuba not scoring a run in a match: 'I don't remember, but it may well have happened'. The USA put their win in perspective when the United States manager, Los Angeles Dodgers' boss Tommy Lasorda, called the win the greatest moment of his life.

Korea won the bronze medal after a play-off with Japan. Australia had hoped to come of age in international baseball, but it won only two out of seven games – one a confidence booster against Korea and the other a lucky win against South Africa. Australia's one standout player was David Nilsson, who topped the leader board on the batting averages and slugging percentage. Nilsson's summation of his team's performance was: 'I think we've given a good effort, but I think we've underachieved'.

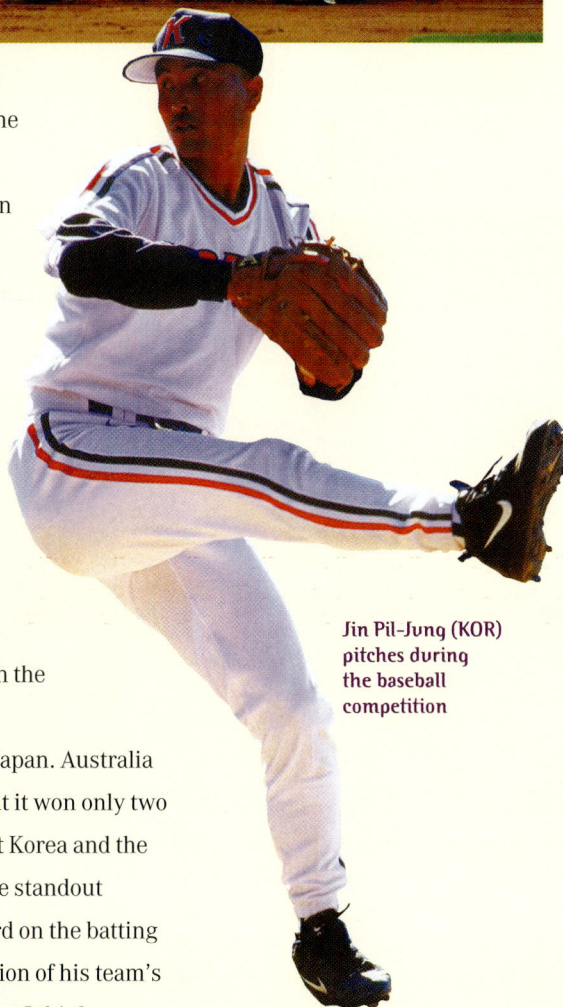
Jin Pil-Jung (KOR) pitches during the baseball competition

See Baseball results on page 93.

USA takes shine off Opals

The USA exerted its supremacy in **women's basketball** with an emphatic gold medal win over the Australian Opals at the Superdome, the score was 76–54. The win ended a valiant campaign by the Australians, but looked almost inevitable when the two teams lined up to play the final. Most of the Americans were head and shoulders above the Australians, and a number of their players such as Sheryl Swoopes, Lisa Leslie, Teresa Edwards and Yolanda Griffith are acknowledged as some of the best in the world.

The Opals had tremendous crowd support and kept carrying the game up to the USA, but, under pressure, shots did not make the basket. Lauren Jackson (AUS), just 19 years of age, showed why she will be the target of American professional clubs in the near future. She played a spirited game, shooting 20 points and collecting 13 rebounds. Inspirational captain Michele Timms, in perhaps her last game for Australia, worked tirelessly and gathered her troops for an emotional huddle after the final siren.

It was all smiles from the Australians, however, when they came out to collect their silver medal. Timms bowed to the crowd and received a thunderous response. It had been a great Olympic Games for Australian women's basketball, and the team had finished with silver, Australia's best-ever result at an Olympic Games.

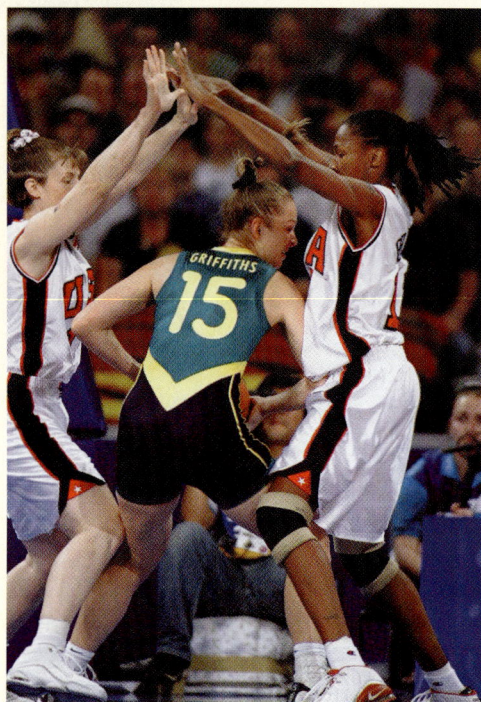

Michelle Griffiths (AUS) in action against the USA in the women's basketball final

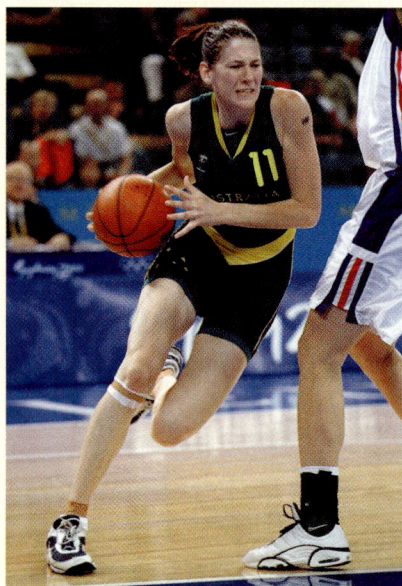

Lauren Jackson (AUS), one of the outstanding players for the Opals

Dream Team triumphs

As expected, the USA took gold in the **men's basketball**. This was the third consecutive gold medal for the American 'Dream Team'; the USA have now won twelve out of fourteen Olympic titles. To achieve this, they have won an amazing 109 of the 111 games they have played in Olympic competition – no mean feat by any standards.

The USA survived a late scare from France and ultimately won 85–75. The real scare for the USA, however, had come in the semifinal, when Lithuania, in the game of the series, came within one basket of beating the USA and toppling the basketball world order.

For the Australians, it had been a hard-fought competition and it seemed that the long careers and campaign of the senior Australians had taken its toll. So it proved as the Australians succumbed to Lithuania in the bronze medal match, 71–89. The icons of the Australian team Andrew Gaze, Luc Longley, Mark Bradtke and Andrew Vlahov have now said it is over, and Shane Heal has hinted at retirement.

The USA celebrate winning gold in the men's basketball

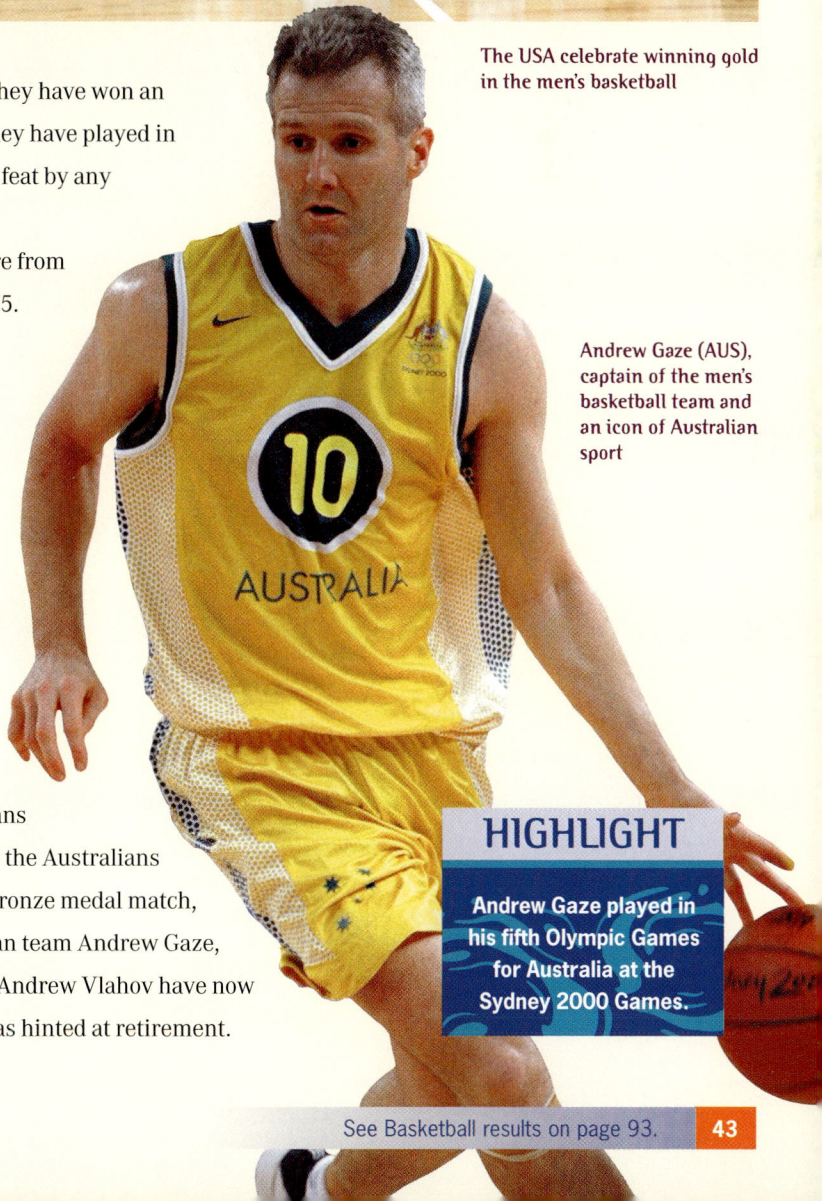

Andrew Gaze (AUS), captain of the men's basketball team and an icon of Australian sport

HIGHLIGHT

Andrew Gaze played in his fifth Olympic Games for Australia at the Sydney 2000 Games.

See Basketball results on page 93.

Savon joins boxing greats

On the brink of victory and his third gold medal in **heavyweight** boxing, Felix Savon (CUB) was suddenly in danger of disqualification. With 15 seconds remaining in the last round, and with victory in the bag against Sultanahmed Ibzagimov (RUS), a cut under Savon's left eye began to bleed heavily. The referee inspected the wound and waved the fight on, allowing Savon to backpedal until the bell. Apart from those final seconds, Savon's win was typically dominant. The 33-year-old used his long reach to stay out of trouble, causing his opponent to swing wildly, and racked up points with his quick fire right and left combinations.

Savon is a six-time world champion and has now won three gold medals in the heavyweight division from three Olympic Games. He is now in the rarified class of Tiefolo Stevenson (CUB) and Hungarian Laslo Pappas. A man of immense presence, he had a few words only for the media: 'I have won to create history for Cuban sport'.

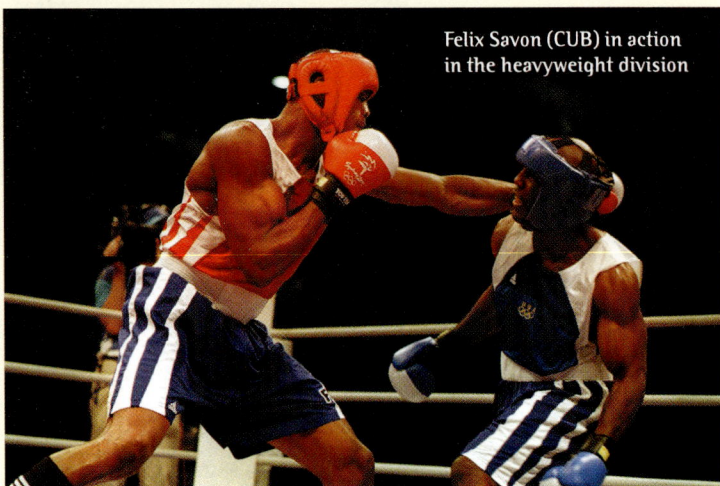

Felix Savon (CUB) in action in the heavyweight division

Felix Savon (CUB) claims gold in the heavyweight division

OLYMPIC FACT

Reginald 'Snowy' Baker won a silver medal for Australia as a boxer in the London Olympic Games of 1908 but also competed in two other events – diving and a freestyle relay.

Cubans scoop medals

The Cubans were a dominant presence in the ring, winning four gold medals and two bronze in the twelve weight divisions. The first Cuban to win on the day of the finals was **bantamweight** Guillermo Rigondeaux Ortiz, who celebrated his twentieth birthday with a win over Raimkoul Malakhbekov (RUS). Rigondeaux was quick moving and continually caught his opponents with jabs. Another Cuban to strike was world champion **lightweight** Mario Kindelan, who kept his rival Andriy Kotelnyk (UKR) at bay. In a close **middleweight** final, Jorge Gutierrez (CUB), outpunched the tough Gaidarbek Gaidarbekov (RUS) late in the last round.

Audley Harrison (GBR) gave his country its first gold medal in boxing since 1968

Great Brit Audley

The Russians also had a successful competition with two gold, three silver and two bronze. Union Jacks waved as Audley Harrison (GBR) gave his country its first gold medal in boxing since the Mexico Olympic Games in 1968. Harrison won the **super-heavyweight** class. At the other end of the weight spectrum, **flyweight** Wijan Ponlid (THA) gave his home nation something to be ecstatic about after taking the gold medal for Thailand, beating Bulat Jumadilov (KAZ).

See Boxing results on pages 93–4.

Canoe/Kayak

Slalom

Whitewater triumph

The European nations dominated the whitewater canoe/kayak competition at Penrith. France and Slovakia each won three medals while the Czech Republic took two medals. A strong second run clinched victory for Stepanka Hilgertova (CZE) over Brigitte Guibal and Anne-Lise Bardet (FRA) in the **women's K1**. In the **men's K1**, Thomas Schmidt (GER) was the gold medallist, winning clearly over Paul Ratcliffe (GBR) and Pierpaolo Ferrazzi (ITA). Tony Estanguet (FRA) won gold in the **men's C1**.

Twins Peter and Pavol Hochschorner (SVK) on their way to gold in the men's C2

Sprint

Hungary for medals

Hungary's four gold medals saw them at the top of the medal table in the Sydney Olympic flatwater competition, finishing with a total of seven medals. Canoe champion Birgit Fischer (GER) became the most successful athlete in canoe/kayak history, after winning two gold medals at the Sydney Olympic Games to take her total medal tally to ten. Thirty-eight-year-old Fischer won gold in the **women's K2 500 metres** and **women's K4 500 metres**, 20 years after winning her first Olympic medal in Moscow. Norway's defending Olympic champion Knut Holmann won gold in the **men's K1 1000 metres** and **K1 500 metres**.

The Australiian paddlers also enjoyed some success in Sydney, winning silver and bronze medals. Daniel Collins and Andrew Trim (AUS) won silver in the **men's K2 500 metres**. They led from the start, but were hauled in by Zoltan Kammerer and Botond Storcz (HUN). Katrin Borchert (AUS) won bronze in the **women's K1 500 metres**, adding to the silver she won at the Barcelona Olympic Games as a member of the K4 500-metre team.

HIGHLIGHT

Slovakian twins Pavol and Peter Hochschorner won gold in the men's C2.

A gold-winning performance from Birgit Fischer and Katrin Wagner (GER) in the women's K2 500 metres

Cycling

Mountain Bike
A day in the bush

It was thrills and spills on the rough bush tracks at Fairfield as the **men's** and **women's mountain bike** events were contested. The slithering, rocky, windy, hilly course included Wombat Crossing, Sheep Paddock Gate, Big Stump and Koala Ridge. Paola Pezzo (ITA) broke away from the bunch in the women's race to successfully defend her Olympic gold from Atlanta, and Miguel Martinez (FRA) left them far behind in the men's event.

Road
Germans dominate

Jan Ullrich (GER), the reigning world time trial champion and winner of the Tour de France in 1997, went out alone three-and-a half kilometres from home in the **men's road race**. This tactic proved successful and he went on to win the gold from Alexandre Vinokourov (KAZ) and Andreas Kloeden (GER). In the **women's road race** there was a desperate dash to the finish. Dutch track star Leontien Zijlaard outsprinted the pack to win by three lengths from Hanka Kupfernagel (GER) and Diana Ziliute (LTU). Australia's Anna Wilson was fourth, missing a medal by the width of a tyre.

The **men's time trial** looked a chance for the great Lance Armstrong (USA), winner of the Tour de France in 2000, but he was denied by Viacheslav Ekimov (RUS) and Jan Ullrich (GER). Leontien Zijlaard (NED), who took gold in the **women's time trial**, enjoyed the most successful Olympic Games of any cyclist – she took three gold and one silver. Anna Wilson (AUS) finished fourth, just six seconds out of the medals.

Miguel Martinez (FRA) negotiates the rocky course in the men's mountain bike event

Leontien Zijlaard (NED) celebrates her win in the women's time trial

See Cycling results on page 95.

Track

Aussie success

Three nations emerged from the Sydney Olympic Games track cycling program with six medals each. France topped the table, with four gold and two silver medals. Germany won two gold, two silver and two bronze medals, while Australia also enjoyed great success winning one gold, two silver and three bronze. In addition to Brett Aitken and Scott McGrory's sensational performance to win gold in the **men's madison**, silver medals went to Michelle Ferris in the **women's 500 m time trial**, and to Gary Neiwand in the **men's keirin**. Bronze medals were won by Brad McGee in the **men's individual pursuit**, Shane Kelly in the **men's time trial**, and the men's team of Sean Eadie, Gary Neiwand and Darryn Hill in the **Olympic sprint**.

Ballanger the legend

Felicia Ballanger (FRA) continued her dominance of track cycling when she won gold in the **women's sprint** and gold in the **women's 500 m time trial** with an Olympic record time of 34.140 seconds. She had previously won the women's match sprint at the Atlanta Games, and has won the world 500 m time trial three times in a row from 1997. She also won the women's individual sprint in the World Championships in 1995 and 1999.

A pumped-up Brad McGee (AUS) after winning the bronze medal in the men's individual pursuit

Felicia Ballanger (FRA) on her way to victory in the women's sprint final

OLYMPIC FACT

The Dunc Gray Velodrome is named in honour of the first Australian to win an Olympic Games or Empire Games cycling medal. Gray won bronze in Amsterdam in 1928 and gold in Los Angeles in 1932 in the 1000 m time trial.

Aitken and McGrory
From heartache to gold

Two cyclists who had experienced their share of personal anguish won Australia's first Olympic track cycling gold medal since 1984, taking out the men's madison on the final night of competition at the Dunc Gray Velodrome.

Brett Aitken's 2-year-old daughter Ashley had experienced medical problems, while Scott McGrory lost his infant son Alexander only three months prior to the Sydney 2000 Games. Both athletes thought of their children as they took gold in a race that often resembled a game of roller derby on bikes.

An emotional McGrory thanked his partner Donna Casey after the win, saying her encouragement had kept him in the sport after their tragedy. Aitken was inspired by a smile from his daughter in the grandstand.

At the World Championships in Berlin in 1999, Aitken had a bad fall in which he dislocated his left shoulder and suffered concussion. McGrory heroically completed the last fifty laps on his own, ensuring the opportunity for himself and Aitken to compete in the madison at the 2000 Olympic Games.

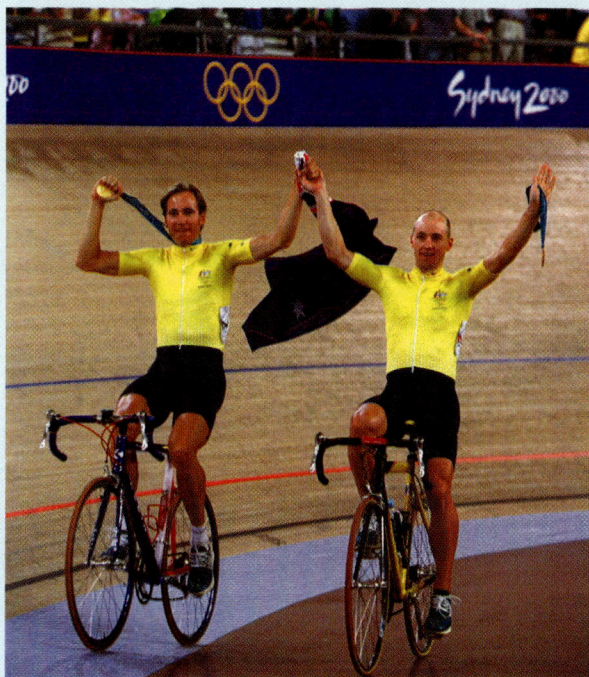

A golden victory in the men's madison for Brett Aitken and Scott McGrory (AUS)

The madison, which made its Olympic debut in Sydney, is a 60-kilometre race that takes its name from the famous Madison Square Garden in New York. Teams of two riders each, work together to accumulate points from a series of sprints, taking turns to sling-shot each other around the track. The Australians combined perfectly. They rode the home crowd support to the full, and managed to accumulate 26 points on a 5–3–2–1 basis in the sprint sections. Only metres from the line, a spectacular crash sent riders flying, but the Australians managed to steer clear and stay on course to win gold.

See Cycling results on page 96.

Dressage
Dressed for gold

The favourites Anky van Grunsven (NED) and her horse Bonfire lived up to expectations in the **individual dressage** final, with a dazzling routine set to a background of dramatic music. The pair scored 239.18 points, to relegate Isabell Werth (GER) and Ulla Salzgeber (GER) to the minor medals. The first and second positions from the Atlanta Games had been reversed. It was a dramatic day for Salzgeber. Her music stopped halfway through the performance, and she was obliged to start again half-an-hour later.

Anky van Grunsven (NED) and Bonfire live up to expectations in the individual dressage

In the **team dressage**, Germany made it five from five with a gold medal performance to match their first placings at the Barcelona Games and the Atlanta Games. Once again, The Netherlands took the silver medal and the USA took the bronze (as they both had done in 1992 and 1996). It was the eighth gold medal for Germany in the team dressage competition since 1964.

Jumping
Netherlands in thriller

Jeroen Dubbeldam (NED) on Sjiem took gold in the **individual jumping**, and Albert Voorn (NED) won silver. Saudi Arabia won its first ever equestrian medal when Khaled Al Eid took bronze. The results were the culmination of difficult times for riders, on a course that was criticised as being slippery and too difficult, and a blustery wind on the final day. In the **team jumping**, Germany narrowly beat Switzerland, with Brazil edging out France in a jump-off for bronze.

Jeroen Dubbeldam (NED) and Sjiem on their way to gold in the individual jumping

Three Day Event

Andrew Hoy, Matt Ryan, Phillip Dutton and Stuart Tinney (AUS) upheld an Australian tradition by winning gold in the team three day event

Australia's golden team

One of the stirring memories of the Sydney Olympic Games will be that of four Australians riding side by side, each bearing an Australian flag, with the packed stands of the Sydney International Equestrian Centre rising to salute them. Andrew Hoy, Matt Ryan, Phillip Dutton and Stuart Tinney (AUS) upheld an Australian tradition by winning the **team three day event** and brought reminders of the glorious back-to-back wins at the Barcelona Games and the Atlanta Games. It was the third gold in a row for Andrew Hoy who had led the team from the front with a brilliant dressage performance on the first day. The team then consolidated its position with a good performance in the cross country. Great Britain posed a threat in the jumping, but it was Hoy's final round that secured victory.

David O'Connor (USA) and Custom Made take the lead in the individual three day event

Silver on Swizzle In

Andrew Hoy (AUS) also won a silver medal in the **individual three day event**, with the result hanging in the balance right to the end. Hoy was fourth entering the jumping round, with David O'Connor (USA) on Custom Made leading the competition. Hoy climbed the leader board with outstanding jumping on Swizzle In, leaving O'Connor to jump last. In a brave performance, O'Connor knocked down only one rail to take the gold.

OLYMPIC FACT

Only military officers were allowed to take part in the first equestrian competition at the modern Olympic Games in 1912.

See Equestrian results on pages 96–7.

Andrew Hoy
Riding high

Super horseman Andrew Hoy (AUS)

Given his distinguished record, it came as no surprise that Andrew Hoy was given the honour of carrying the Australian flag at the opening ceremony of the Atlanta Games in 1996.

Andrew Hoy's superstatus as a horseman and Olympian owes its beginnings to his family farm in New South Wales. 'I was chasing sheep and cattle from a young age', says Hoy. 'I also did pony club, campdrafting and rodeo, but I had a limited career there as I found it difficult to stay on for eight seconds.' The experience gave him the grounding, however, for elite competition in one of the world's most dangerous sports, equestrian events and showjumping.

Hoy is a veteran of the equestrian world. In 1980, at the age of 21, he was picked for the Olympic Games in Moscow, but in the atmosphere of boycott, the equestrian authorities decided not to field a team.

Hoy finally went to his first Olympic Games in Los Angeles in 1984, and then to Seoul in 1988, finishing fifth in team events in both cities. He took his horse Kiwi to the Barcelona Games in 1992, where he teamed with Gillian Rolton, Matt Ryan and David Green to win gold in the team three day event. It came as no surprise when Hoy won his second gold medal at the Atlanta Games, with teammates Gillian Rolton, Wendy Schaefer and Phillip Dutton.

After a third gold medal in successive games, the softly spoken Hoy is not quite finished yet. Athens in 2004? 'Why not?' he says.

See Equestrian results on pages 96–7.

Fencing

Italy tops medals

Italy topped the fencing competition winning three gold medals in a five-medal haul. France also won six medals, with one gold. The fencing competition, featuring individual and team foil, épée and sabre competitions is one of only four sports that has been held at every Olympic Games.

The Russians claimed gold in the men's team with a convincing win over France

Korean takes gold

Young-Ho Kim (KOR) temporarily moved the Europeans off centre stage at the fencing when he won the gold medal in the **men's individual foil**, beating Ralf Bissdorf (GER). In the tense third round of the final bout, Kim took a 14–10 lead and seemed a clear winner, but Bissdorf scored four crucial touches, bringing the score to 14–14. Kim landed his winning point in the final moment to become the first Korean to win a gold medal in fencing. One of the most convincing wins of the competition was that of the Russian Federation team in the **men's team sabre**. They overwhelmed opponents France, winning seven of the nine bouts and drawing the remaining two.

In the **women's individual foil**, Valentina Vezzali (ITA) added gold to her individual silver and team gold from the Atlanta Olympic Games. Italy also took gold in the **women's team foil**.

A jubilant Italian team after winning gold in the women's team foil

See Fencing results on page 97.

The Lion Kings

With a crowd of over 98 000 roaring its support, the underdogs of the **men's football** final, Cameroon, pulled off a stunning victory over Spain. The match came down to a penalty shoot-out, during which the full weight of soccer history fell on the shoulders of Cameroon striker Pierre Wome. Spanish defender Amaya had hit the crossbar when taking his penalty shot and it was all up to Wome. He held his nerve and shot truly. The crowd went wild as the men in green, red and yellow danced and embraced. It was Cameroon's first ever Olympic gold medal.

Early in the match, the Spanish team scored from a free kick. A few minutes later they were threatening to make the score 2–0, when Cameroon's 16-year-old goalie Idriss Carlos Kameni made a great save. Cameroon then began to play with flair, but often gave the ball away with poor passing. Then Spain scored a second goal and went into half-time two up.

Cameroon was a revitalised side in the second half, playing with enormous dash and courage. They scored in the fifty-third minute, and two minutes later Samuel Eto'o Fils scored from a great cross. Spain tried hard to stop them, and had two players sent off the field. Cameroon bombarded the goals, but Spain's defence was impressive and they held on to force extra time. The scores remained deadlocked after extra time, forcing the climactic penalty shoot-out. In the end, the axis of world soccer tilted towards Cameroon. They were the pride of Africa.

Cameroon's football team celebrates its stunning victory over Spain to claim the gold medal

Daniel Ngom Kome (CMR) is challenged by Lacruz (ESP) during the final of the men's football

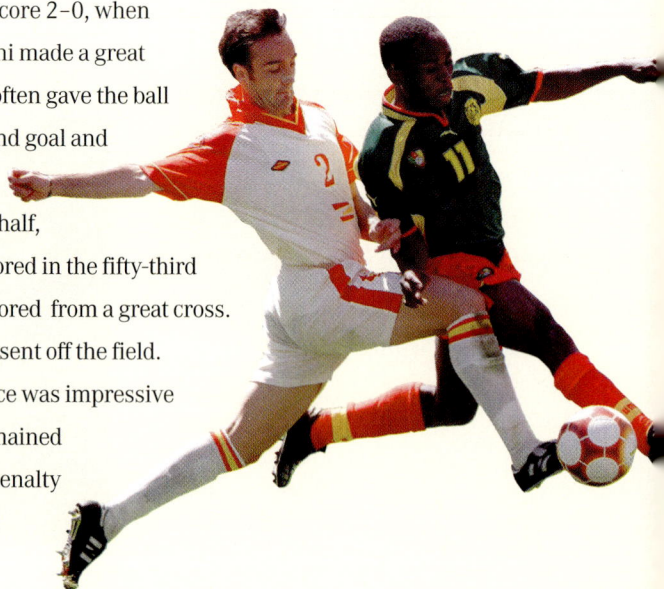

Chile takes bronze

The surprise packet of the **men's football** was the USA, which forced its way into the bronze medal match. Despite looking the better side for much of the game, the USA eventually went down to Chile, a side that had played some exciting football in the preceding games of the tournament. The final score was 2–0. The Olyroos (AUS) battled bravely in the opening match at the Melbourne Cricket Ground until a late goal brought them undone by Italy. Further on in the competition, Australia was beaten by Honduras and defending champions Nigeria.

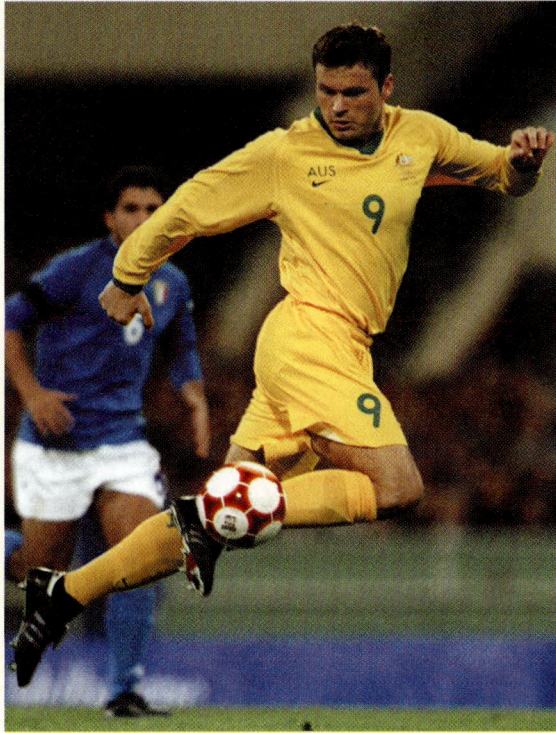

Mark Viduka (AUS) in action against Italy in a preliminary football match

Golden extra for Norway

The final of the **women's football** was an epic contest. Norway and the USA played for the gold medal in an exciting match. With less than a minute before the final whistle, the USA scored an equalising goal to force the match into extra time. Under pressure, Norwegian substitute Dagny Mellgren scored the winning goal to down the defending champions. Germany defeated Brazil 2–0 to win the bronze medal. The highlight of the Matildas' (AUS) Sydney campaign was Sunni Hughes (AUS) scoring what was rated the goal of the tournament against the powerful Brazilians.

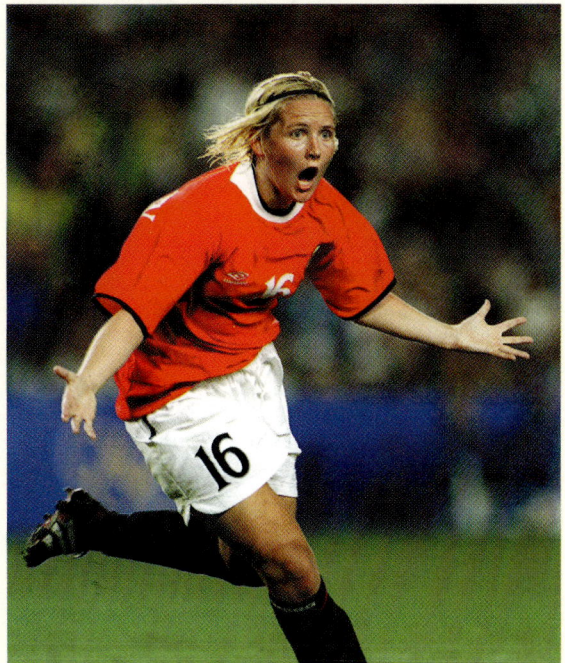

Ragnhild Gulbrandsen (NOR) celebrates a goal in the final of the women's football

See Football results on page 97.

Gymnastics
Artistic

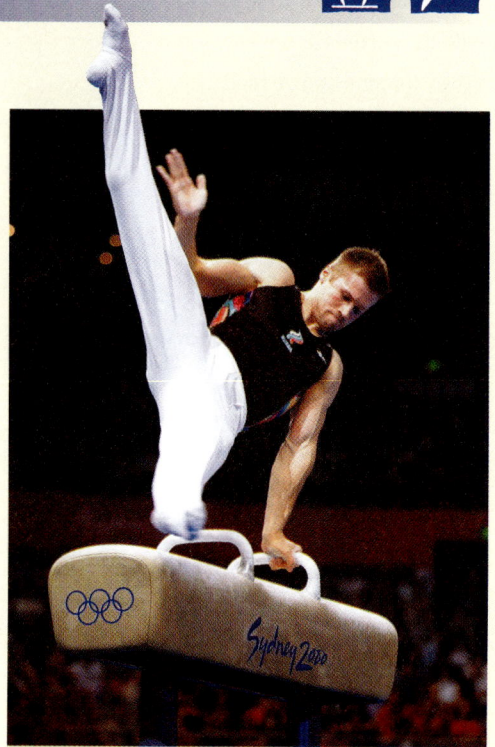

Artistic Alexei

The men's artistic gymnastic events saw great performances from the 24-year-old Alexei Nemov (RUS), who came into the competition with six medals from the Atlanta Games, including gold in the men's team event and individual vault. At the Sydney Olympic Games, he put it all together winning the **men's individual all-round** title, and scored best in the **men's team** event helping his team to a bronze medal. In the men's individual events he also took gold in the **horizontal bar**, silver in the **floor exercise**, bronze in the **pommel horse** and bronze in the **parallel bars**. Despite the stern demeanour of some of the gymnasts, Nemov has been dubbed a playboy. His comment was: 'We are all just ordinary people. Sometimes you go to bed at 2 am, sometimes you want to have a beer after the competition, so that is part of my lifestyle too'. Igors Vihrovs (LAT) won Latvia's first Olympic gold medal, edging out Nemov in the **men's floor exercise**.

Alexei Nemov (RUS) impressed with his style winning the men's individual all-round title

Golden bars

The powerful Chinese team won the **men's team** event from the Ukraine and the Russian Federation, despite only scoring one gold medal in the individual competition. It was Li Xiaopeng (CHN) who took gold on the **men's parallel bars**. Australian Philippe Rizzo, 19, was advised just before the event's commencement that he was included in the men's individual all-round competition. His performance was highlighted by a world-class 9.750 on the horizontal bar, and a personal best score of 55.786.

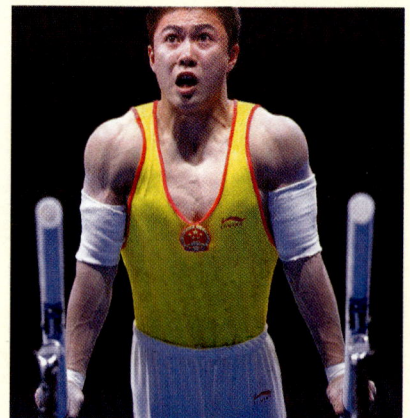

Li Xiaopeng (CHN) took gold on the men's parallel bars

Triumph turns sour

The intensity of the Olympic artistic gymnastics boiled over from the climax of competition to an unseemly row over drug taking and a disqualification. The drama centred around a tablet containing pseudo-ephedrine, administered to 16- year-old gymnast Andreea Raducan (ROM). The Romanian was the best of the elegant young women who went through the **women's individual all-round competition** of beam, floor exercise, uneven bars and vault. An explosive package, Raducan scored 9.706 points on the vault, 9.825 on the floor, 9.575 on uneven bars and a brilliant 9.787 on the beam. Trailing in her wake, but collecting the silver and bronze medals were teammates Simona Amanar (ROM) and Maria Olaru (ROM).

Andreea Raducan's (ROM) triumph turned to tragedy when she was disqualified in the individual all-round competition

Raducan's golden triumph soon changed to heartbreak, when her disqualification was announced. Amanar and Olaru went up in the medal rankings and Liu Xuan (CHN) was added in third place. Australian Lisa Skinner, who put in an outstanding performance, was elevated from ninth to eighth. Romania took the case to the Court of Arbitration of Sport but lost the appeal against the ruling. Raducan was allowed to keep her gold medal in the **women's team** event and silver in the **women's vault** that she had also won in the Games.

The Romanian team received gold in the women's team event

See Gymnastics results on pages 98–9.

Swinging into gear

Elena Zamolodtchikova (RUS) won gold in the **women's individual floor exercise** and the vault while Liu Xuan (CHN) won the **beam**. Svetlana Khorkina (RUS), the 21-year-old four-time world champion, was a surprise failure in the individual all-round competition. The fact that the vault had been set at an incorrect height for the first two rotations may have been a contributing factor. She recovered to take gold in the **uneven bars** and silver in the **floor exercise**. The **women's team** events medals went to Romania, the Russian Federation and China.

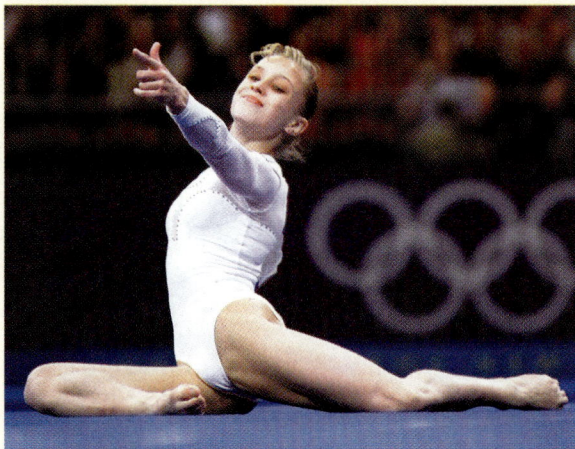

Elena Zamolodtchikova (RUS), gold medallist in the women's individual floor exercise

Rhythmic
Fascinating rhythm

Disappointed with their bronze medal in Atlanta, the Russians formed a completely new rhythmic gymnastic team, comprised of Irina Belova, Elena Chalamova, Natalia Lavrova, Maria Netessova, Irina Zilber and Vera Shimanskaya. Their decision was rewarded with a gold medal. The **group competition** involved team members using hoops and ribbons, and then clubs in a display of rhythmic movement set to music. The Russian Federation won by presenting an unconventional clubs routine, performed to a modern, up-tempo piece of music.

The highly drilled Greek team went into the final as top qualifiers, but dropped a club in their first routine and finished third. The crowd favourite was the Brazilian team, whose racy routines brought great acclaim. There was audible disappointment at the low Brazilian scores.

The Brazilian team were a crowd favourite in the group competition

 See Gymnastics results on pages 98–9.

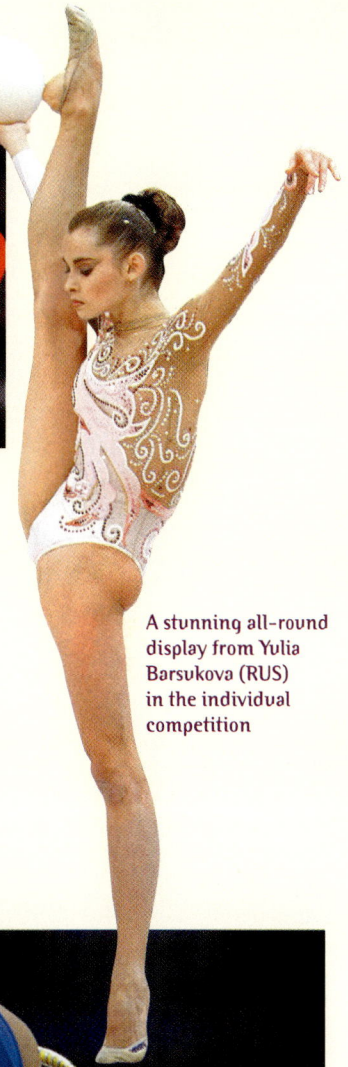

A stunning all-round display from Yulia Barsukova (RUS) in the individual competition

Barsukova is best

The 1999 world champion Alina Kabaeva (RUS) was in the lead when she committed a major blunder in the **individual competition**, causing what observers described as the biggest upset of the gymnastics competition at the Sydney Olympic Games. Kabaeva threw the hoop over her head, but lost control and had to retrieve it outside the competition area. That incurred an automatic penalty, and despite strong performances with the ball, rope and ribbon, she had to settle for the bronze medal. Yulia Barsukova (RUS) took the gold medal after a strong all-round display, while Yulia Raskina (BLR) won silver.

Trampoline

Wallace takes silver

Ji Wallace (AUS) was definitely the most excited man in Australia when he won a silver medal in the inaugural **men's trampoline**. The 23-year-old kept punching the air and saying: 'I can't believe it. Oh, my god. Oh, my god'. Long after the other competitors had left the floor, Wallace was still out there, clutching his medal and basking in the occasion.

Wallace was the top scorer after five of the eight finalists had completed their routines. He then had to wait for the top three to go through. The first two fell below his score and as world champion Alexandre Moskalenko (RUS) stepped up to the trampoline, he was all that stood between Ji and gold. Moskalenko showed his class, however, pulling off a brilliant routine to win by a wide margin. The bronze went to Mathieu Turgeon (CAN).

An excited Ji Wallace (AUS) with his silver medal in the inaugural men's trampoline

Historic win

The first-ever Olympic gold medal in trampoline was won by Irina Karavaeva (RUS) in the **women's trampoline**. The three-time world champion claimed the historic medal with a mark of 38.90. The silver medal was won by Oxana Tsyhuleva (UKR) and the bronze by Karen Cockburn (CAN).

The gold medal for the women's trampoline was won by Irina Karavaeva (RUS)

HIGHLIGHT

The man who developed the sport and equipment for trampolining, 86-year-old American George Nissen, was in the crowd to see the event.

See Gymnastics results on pages 98–9.

Top nations meet again

The Russian Federation and Sweden are the leading nations in **men's handball**, a game that is little known in Australia. In the final, the Russian men's team won its fourth Olympic title, denying the Swedes the double title of world and Olympic champions. The match was of a high standard, fast-paced and featuring strong attacking and robust defence. Both goal keepers were kept busy: Russian Federation captain Andrei Lavrov made nine saves, while Sweden's Tomas Svensson was also in wonderful touch. The full house at The Dome was backing Sweden, who led 14–13 at half time, but the Russians went on a blitz early in the second term, scoring seven straight goals. The Russian Federation won 28–26. Spain took the bronze medal in men's handball defeating Yugoslavia 26–22.

Magnus Wislander (SWE) shoots during the men's handball final

Danes roar back

In the **women's handball**, defending Olympic champion Denmark came from behind in dramatic circumstances to beat Hungary 31–27. With just 15 minutes to go, the Hungarians led by six goals, but the Danes came roaring back. They scored fourteen goals in that short space of time, limiting Hungary to just three scoring shots. Anette Hoffmann Moberg (DEN) and Camilla Andersen (DEN) were the attacking weapons that gave the Danes the gold medal. Norway defeated South Korea 22–21 to win bronze.

The women's handball final was played out between Hungary and Denmark

See Handball results on page 99.

Hockey

Legendary Hockeyroos

Australia's **women's hockey** team ended a magnificent Olympic tournament, beating a gallant Argentina 3–1. The Hockeyroos (AUS) came through the tournament with flying colours beating The Netherlands 5–0, Korea 3–0, China 5–1 and drawing with Spain 1–1. In the final, they quickly established their supremacy to lead 3–0. A second-half goal in a spirited fightback by Argentina created a little tension, but the Australians lifted with some good defensive work, and then it was over. The Australians leapt for joy. They gathered in a tight circle, displaying the close-knit comradeship that had carried them through many years of training and travelling together. The Netherlands took bronze from their match against Spain.

Katie Allen (AUS) focuses on the ball in the women's hockey final

Golden double

The Netherlands successfully defended its Olympic title in the **men's hockey**, becoming the first side to achieve this feat in 44 years. The Dutch were up against Korea, and the scores were deadlocked 3–3 at the end of full-time. Extra time produced no results and it came down to a penalty shoot-out. The Dutch held their nerve to win 5–4.

The Dutch celebrate their victory over Korea in the men's hockey

The Australian Kookaburras made the semifinals and came up against the powerful Dutch team. The match was extremely tight, and when full-time sounded, it went into two periods of extra time. There was still no breakthrough, so it came down to a penalty shoot-out. After four shots, the scores were still even. The Dutch keeper then saved Australia's fifth shot to win the match. In the play-off for third and fourth, Australia won the bronze medal with a 6–3 victory over Pakistan.

The Hockeyroos
Back-to-back gold

The Australian women's hockey team after winning gold over Argentina

Of all the Olympic teams in all the sports, the Hockeyroos must rank as the most outstanding. They have not lost a major tournament since Ric Charlesworth took over as coach in 1993. The win in Sydney was their second consecutive Olympic gold medal, and their third in four Olympic Games.

Rechelle Hawkes was ecstatic after the Hockeyroos' win over Argentina. In addition to being part of Australia's most successful team, she had just joined swimming legend Dawn Fraser and equestrian star Andrew Hoy as a gold medallist at three Olympic Games. Hawkes also had the great honour of reading the athlete's oath at the opening ceremony of the Sydney Olympic Games.

Victory was sweet also for goal scorer Jenny Morris. She was one of the stars at the Atlanta Games, but seemed unlikely to get back into the team after a serious knee injury. Such is the spirit of the Hockeyroos that she gave herself the role of team 'gopher', assisting in any way she could, while she worked on her rehabilitation.

The first goal of the gold medal game was scored by Alyson Annan, who had been the star of the series, a star in a team where competitiveness and skill was spread evenly from the front to the back. The second goal came from Juliet Haslam and the third from Jenny Morris. It was time to celebrate!

The Hockeyroos rejoiced in style before a crowd of 15 000 spectators bedecked in green and gold, geed up by cheerleader Lawrie Lawrence. John Williamson's 'Waltzing Matilda' was sung many times over as the team delighted in their victory. It was a fitting end to Ric Charlesworth's remarkable coaching career and another golden moment for the Hockeyroos.

See Hockey results on page 99.

Judo

Pekli takes bronze

Australia's Maria Pekli overcame a painful knee injury to win a bronze medal in the **women's 57 kilogram** judo event. The 28-year-old represented Hungary at the 1992 and 1996 Olympic Games, but was competing for the host nation when she took to the mat in Sydney. When the Melbourne student won bronze, the jubilant crowd almost lifted the roof off the Sydney Exhibition Centre – this was Australia's first Olympic medal in judo since 1964. Isabel Fernandez (ESP) took gold and Driulys Gonzalez (CUB) won silver.

Japan's gold rush

It was Japan who dominated the judo competition, winning four gold, two silver and two bronze medals from the fourteen events held in Sydney. Japan took gold in the **men's 60 kilogram**, **81 kilogram** and **100 kilogram** classes and the **women's 48 kilogram** class. France was the next most successful nation with six medals, ahead of Cuba with five medals.

Maria Pekli (AUS) throws Cinzia Cavazzuti (ITA) during the women's 57 kilogram judo event

OLYMPIC FACT

Judo developed in Japan in the late 19th century, so it was fitting that the sport was first included at the Tokyo Olympic Games in 1964.

Kosei Inoue (JPN) celebrates his gold medal success in the men's 100 kilogram judo event

See Judo results on pages 99–100.

Modern Pentathlon

Late run for Russian in pentathlon

Dmitry Svatkovsky (RUS) gradually overhauled the field to win the **men's modern pentathlon**. Svatkovsky was back in the pack in the early rounds, and started the final event, a 3000-metre run, in fifth place. He completed the run in 9:21.79 to win the gold over Gabor Balogh (HUN) and Pavel Dovgal (BLR). The modern pentathlon tests athletes in five disciplines: shooting, fencing, swimming, equestrian and running. In shooting, air pistols are used to fire 20 shots from 10 metres; in fencing, athletes fence every other competitor with épées; in swimming, competitors complete a time trial of 200 metres; and in equestrian, they must ride unfamiliar horses through a showjumping round. Only twenty-four competitors took part in the event, with the host country having one entrant.

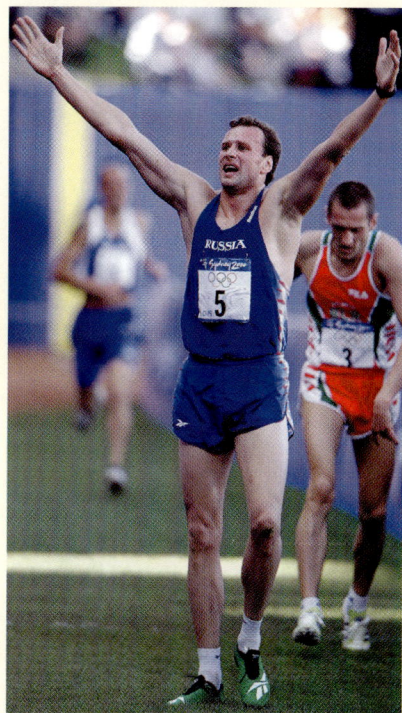

A thrilling win for Dmitry Svatkovsky (RUS) in the men's modern pentathlon

Cook runs down rivals

The inaugural **women's modern pentathlon** gold medal was decided in thrilling circumstances, and mirrored the finish in the men's competition. Stephanie Cook (GBR) was back in eighth place after four events, and started the run 49 seconds behind Emily deRiel (USA) and 44 seconds behind her British teammate Kate Allenby. But she ran down the two leaders, passing deRiel with only 300 metres to go, and claimed the gold medal. The American took silver, while Allenby won the bronze.

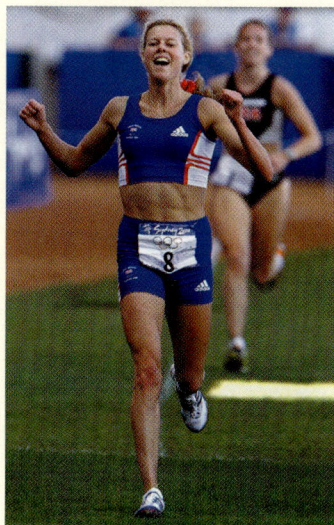

Stephanie Cook (GBR) runs down her opponents in the women's modern pentathlon

OLYMPIC FACT

The modern pentathlon was invented by the founder of the modern Olympic Games, Baron Pierre de Coubertin, who included it in the Olympic program in Stockholm in 1912.

See Modern Pentathlon results on page 100.

Rowing

Romania tops tally

Expectations were high for Australia's rowing team, as they had won two gold, one silver and one bronze medal in Atlanta, and had the advantage of being on home waters. Everything was going to plan when eleven crews reached the finals in the fourteen events contested. But this was a tough competition, and the close and exciting races kept the big crowds at the Penrith course bubbling with excitement. Romania ended the competition on top of the medal table with three gold, but it was Germany who had the depth in their line-up collecting two gold, one silver and three bronze. Australia had to be content with three silver and two bronze.

A jubilant Rachael Taylor and Kate Slatter (AUS) after winning silver in the women's coxless pair

Battles to the line

Australia's **women's coxless pair** of Rachael Taylor and Kate Slatter finished second, while the **men's coxless pair** of Matthew Long and James Tomkins (formerly of the 'Oarsome Foursome' coxless four) won a bronze behind France and the USA.

Simon Burgess, Anthony Edwards, Darren Balmforth and Robert Richards (AUS) going for broke in the men's lightweight coxless four

The premier event, the **men's eight**, was a tremendous battle to the line, with Australia coming second to Great Britain. Australia's crew was Christian Ryan, Alastair Gordon, Nick Porzig, Robert Jahrling, Mike McKay, Stuart Welch, Daniel Burke, Jaime Fernandez and Brett Hayman. In the **men's lightweight coxless four** there was gold in the offing for Simon Burgess, Anthony Edwards, Darren Balmforth and Robert Richards, but the crew was pipped on the line by France.

> **OLYMPIC FACT**
>
> **Australian Olympic single sculls champion Merv Wood went to four Olympic Games, winning one gold, one silver and one bronze medal.**

Super Steven

The new Australian **men's coxless four** of James Stewart, Ben Dodwell, Geoff Stewart and Bo Hanson rowed a fabulous race, but lost to Great Britain and Italy. This was a highlight of the regatta and one of the British crew was Steven Redgrave, who won his fifth consecutive Olympic gold medal. Redgrave started at Los Angeles in the coxed four, and won in a coxless pair at the Seoul, Barcelona and Atlanta Games. His 1992 and 1996 partner Matthew Pinsent was in the winning crew with Redgrave in Sydney. International Olympic Committee President Juan Antonio Samaranch, presented Redgrave with a special gold pin to acknowledge his remarkable achievement.

Great Britain's men's coxless four, James Cracknell, Steven Redgrave, Tim Foster and Matthew Pinsent (not pictured), are presented with their gold medals

Champion rowers

In a dominant display in the **women's eight**, Romania, the world and Olympic champions, beat The Netherlands for gold, while Canada took bronze. Elisabeta Lipa (ROM) took home her fourth Olympic gold medal after having won medals in 1984, 1992 and 1996. The women's eight was a second gold medal for Georgeta Damian (ROM) and Doina Ignat (ROM), who also won gold in the **women's coxless pair**.

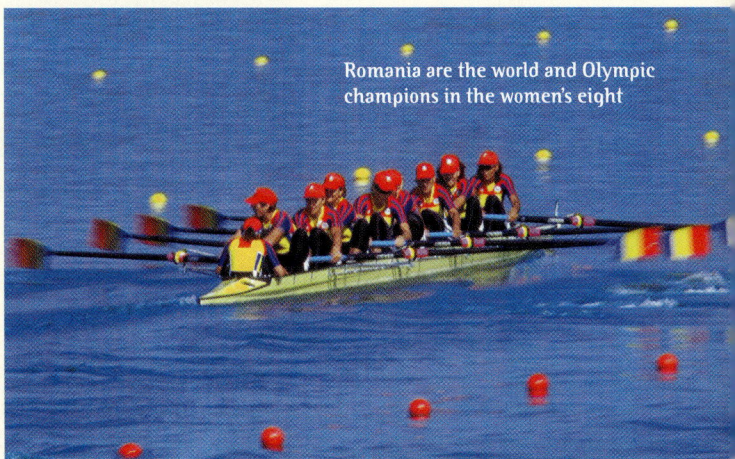

Romania are the world and Olympic champions in the women's eight

Close call

The closest race of the regatta was the **women's single sculls**, after which there was a long wait while judges decided the result. In the end they awarded the race to Ekaterina Karsten (BLR) by one hundredth of a second over Rumyana Neykova (BUL).

OLYMPIC FACT

Hungarian fencer Aladar Gerevich is the only athlete to win more gold medals at consecutive Olympic Games than Steven Redgrave. Gerevich achieved his six gold medals in fencing between 1932 and 1960.

See Rowing results on pages 100–1.

Sailing thrills

The harbour was the visual jewel of the Olympic Games – the Sydney Harbour Bridge, the Sydney Opera House and the sparkling expanse of water making a beautiful backdrop for the many television pictures

Mark Reynolds and Magnus Liljedahl (USA) sailing to gold in the open star class

beamed around the world. It was also the perfect place to watch the Olympic competition, and spectators found vantage points right around the harbour. The glorious weather that blessed the Games did not help the sailors, however, and many events in the nine different classes of boats, were delayed and rescheduled as the light airs thwarted really challenging competition.

Spinnaker magic

Sailing hit the front page on 28 September, when Australia won two gold medals within two hours. Firstly, Jenny Armstrong and Belinda Stowell (AUS) won the **women's 470**. Armstrong and Stowell nearly came to grief early. The pair almost missed the start in the first race when they became squeezed on the line

Jenny Armstrong and Belinda Stowell (AUS) stretch their lead in the women's 470 final

next to the committee boat, but the two sailed strongly in the competition and they went to the final race in the lead. They stretched their lead further in the final race, and had an exhilarating run to the line to take gold. The USA won silver and the Ukraine took bronze.

Aussies clinch victory

Tom King and Mark Turnbull (AUS) won the **men's 470**, clinching Australia's second gold medal in sailing. They needed a top-five finish in the final race to make sure the American crew could not overtake them, and their second placing assured them of victory. The pair had to battle difficult moments in the second race, hitting the mark on a turn and being the victim of one of the many wind shifts that dogged the competition. The success of the 470 crews was a tribute to their hard work, but part of the credit must go to the coaching of Victor Kovalenko. Kovalenko also coached the Ukrainian 470 crews to a gold and a bronze in the Atlanta Games.

Sailing duo Mark Turnbull and Tom King (AUS) celebrate after winning the gold medal in the men's 470 class

Brits ride wave of success

Ben Ainslie (GBR) won the gold medal in the **open laser**, with Michael Blackburn (AUS) taking third. It was Great Britain's second gold in a day, after Shirley Robertson (GBR) held off a challenge from Margriet Matthysse (NED) to win gold in the **women's Europe**. Great Britain made sure it was the most successful sailing nation at the Sydney Olympic Games when Iain Percy (GBR) secured gold in the **men's finn**. Australia won a silver medal in the **open tornado**, when Darren Bundock and John Forbes (AUS) sailed to a last-race victory. The gold went to the former world champions, Roman Hagara and Hans Pieter Steinacher (AUT). The USA took the gold medal in the **open star** class when Mark Reynolds and Magnus Liljedahl grabbed the title in the last race of the competition.

A glorious victory for Ben Ainslie (GBR) in the open laser class

See Sailing results on page 101.

China shoots to the front

The shooting competition was divided into seventeen events: ten for men and seven for women. Events were in four categories: shot gun (clay target), rifle, pistol and running target.

China emerged on top of the table, with three gold, two silver and three bronze. Russia won a total of six medals (one gold, three silver and two bronze) but was placed behind Bulgaria and Sweden (two gold medals each). Australia was ranked fifth, with one gold, one silver and one bronze.

Triumph for Aussies

Michael Diamond defended his Olympic **men's trap** title with an emotional victory, dedicated to his late father. The reigning world champion always looked in control, hitting every target during the final. Ian Peel (GBR) took the silver and Giovanni Pellielo (ITA) won bronze.

Winners in the women's 10-metre air pistol event: Jasna Sekaric (YUG) silver, Tao Luna (CHN) gold, Annemarie Forder (AUS) bronze

Russell Mark, who won the **men's double trap** gold in Atlanta, led into the final section of the event in Sydney. The 36-year-old Victorian was in great form, but a two shot lead disappeared at the range at Cecil Park, and Mark found himself in a nail-biting shoot-off with Richard Faulds (GBR). Twice Shooter of the Year in Britain, Faulds was icy cool in the finish and won gold; Mark took silver.

Annemarie Forder completed Australia's shooting medals. The Queenslander produced the performance of a lifetime to take bronze in the **women's 10-metre air pistol** event.

Sharp shooter, Russell Mark (AUS)

See Shooting results on page 102.

Michael Diamond
Australia's top gun

Michael Diamond (AUS) aims for gold

A jubilant Michael Diamond (AUS) after the medal ceremony

According to Michael Diamond, it was the love and support of his late father that helped him retain his Olympic title and win Australia's third gold medal of the Games.

The 28-year-old kept his emotions in check throughout the gruelling competition played out on the rolling hills of Cecil Park. He missed only three targets in 150 shots ending up with an overall score of 147 out of a possible 150. Even though Diamond was unable to better his own Olympic record of 149 points out of 150, it was still enough to bring home the gold.

But when it was over, he tearfully embraced his mother, as they both remembered Diamond's father, coach and long-time mentor who died in May this year.

'This was for dad,' said Diamond, who was taught to shoot by his father. 'It was my first major event without him, and I thought he didn't teach me for twenty years for me to walk out there and fail at such a big event.'

Diamond, who enjoys relaxing on the beach in his leisure time, has a string of major titles to his credit. Some of the highlights include gold in the men's trap at the World Cup held in Hiroshima, Japan in 1995, and numerous other international titles. Diamond also took gold in the men's trap in the Atlanta Olympic Games in 1996. To successfully defend his Olympic title had always been a dream. Winning in front of a home crowd made the victory extra special.

See Shooting results on page 102.

Softball

Hot sport for Aussies

Softball became a hot sport for Australian spectators at the Sydney Olympic Games. Thanks to the big hitting of Peta Edebone (AUS), the team had a successful run to the semifinals and eventually won a bronze medal. Edebone is the vice-captain and a team veteran, having played more than 100 games for Australia. The Australian and American teams slugged it out in their first meeting in the competition until Edebone clouted a two-run homer at the bottom of the thirteenth. The Australians won six of their seven preliminary games to get to the semifinals. There was no reprieve here and the Japanese won 1–0 to advance to the gold medal game.

USA hang in for top spot

In the end, the United States team had to work very hard for the gold medal it was expected to claim by right. The USA opened their Olympic campaign with standard wins over Canada and Cuba and then lost three games in a row. Japan and China beat them and then Australia were 2–1 winners in a game that went well past the regulation number of innings. The Americans pulled themselves together, winning two games to get to the final, including a win over Australia in the semifinal. The gold medal was decided by an error. Japan scored at the top of the fourth innings, but the USA equalised, and then scored the winning run on a dropped outfield catch in the eighth innings.

Peta Edebone (AUS) is congratulated by her teammates after hitting a two-run homer against the USA

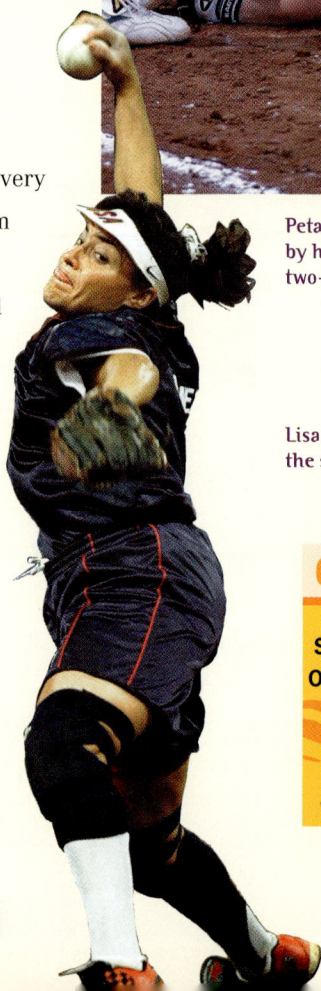

Lisa Fernandez (USA) pitches during the softball final against Japan

OLYMPIC FACT

Softball was introduced to Olympic competition at the Atlanta Games in 1996, where Australia gave notice of its skill by winning a bronze medal.

Table Tennis

China wins table tennis again

China has dominated the table tennis competition since its was introduced on the Olympic program in Seoul in 1988. There were no surprises when they won both the men's and women's singles and doubles at the Sydney Olympic Games. China won four gold medals, three silver medals and one bronze medal. The **men's singles** final was a closely contested affair, and Chinese top seed Kong Linghui had to fight hard for the gold against Jan-Ove Waldner (SWE). Waldner lost the first two games but levelled with strong offensive play in games three and four. Then Kong grabbed an early advantage in the decider and went on to win the match.

Kong Linghui (CHN) on his way to gold in the men's singles final

Doubles pair in singles final

In the **women's singles** final the world No. 1, Wang Nan (CHN), clashed with her doubles partner and world No. 2 Li Ju (CHN), after they had taken gold together in the **women's doubles**. Wang took the first game, but Li won the second and third to edge in front. Wang bounced back, winning the fourth game, to set up the decider. Tension was high as they went point for point, but at 12–12, Wang took the upper hand and went on to claim her second gold medal.

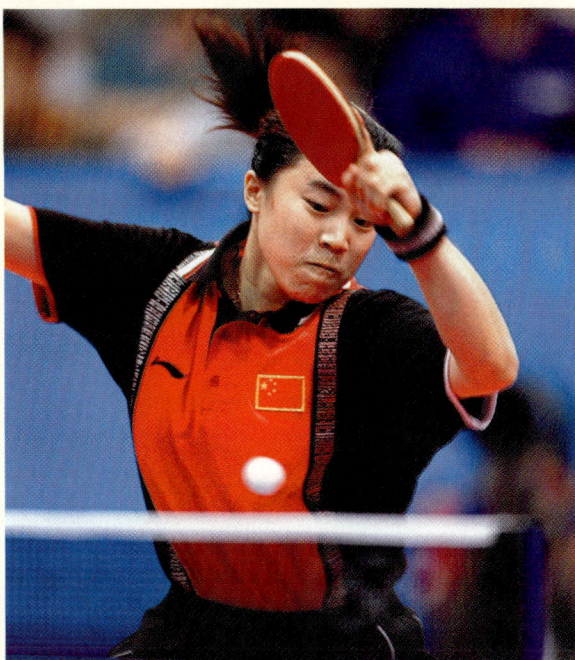

Wang Nan (CHN) beat her doubles partner Li Ju (CHN) on her way to gold in the women's singles final

See Table Tennis results on page 103.

Lauren Burns (AUS) acknowledges the crowd after winning gold in the women's less than 49 kilogram class

A smashing success

Taekwondo's successful debut in Olympic competition was helped along by Lauren Burns (AUS) who won the first gold medal awarded in the sport. The daughter of former pop star Ronnie Burns was ecstatic about her win. To claim the medal, she beat Urbia Melendez Rodriguez (CUB), 4–2, in the **women's less than 49 kilogram** class. Korea took the gold medal in both the **women's 49–57 kilogram** and **women's 57–67 kilogram**. The final event of the Olympic taekwondo competition was the **women's 67+ kilogram**, where Chen Zhong (CHN) was a comfortable winner over Natalia Ivanova (RUS).

Trenton's triumph

Australia's taekwondo medal haul continued in the men's events where Daniel Trenton (AUS) scored a silver medal in the **men's 80+ kilogram**, after a tough match against Kim Kyong-Hun (KOR). In the **men's less than 58 kilogram** contest, Michail Mouroutsos (GRE) was too strong for Gabriel Esparza (ESP), while Steven Lopez (USA) won gold in the **men's 58–68 kilogram** class; Korea's Sin Joon-Sik took silver. The gold medal for the **men's 68–80 kilogram** was taken out by Angel Valodia Matos Fuentes (CUB).

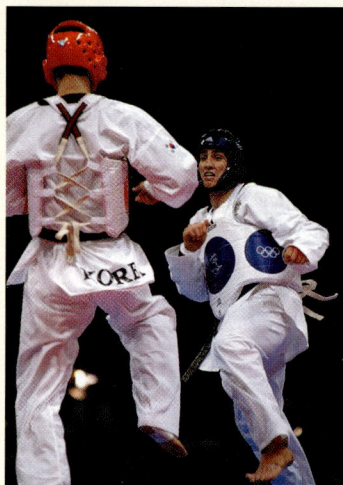

Kim Kyong-Hun (KOR) beat Daniel Trenton (AUS) to take gold in the men's 80+ kilogram

Tennis

Sisters' clean sweep

Powerhouse American Venus Williams made short work of Elena Dementieva (RUS) in the **women's singles** gold medal match. Williams took just 55 minutes to crush Dementieva 6–2, 6–4. It was Williams's thirty-second consecutive victory, and she became the first woman since Germany's Steffi Graf to hold the Wimbledon and US Open titles while taking out the Olympic gold medal. The women's tournament progressed to an all-American, all-Williams affair, as Venus teamed up with her sister Serena to win the **women's doubles**. They beat the Dutch pair of Kristie Boogert and Miriam Oremans 6–1, 6–1 in just 49 minutes.

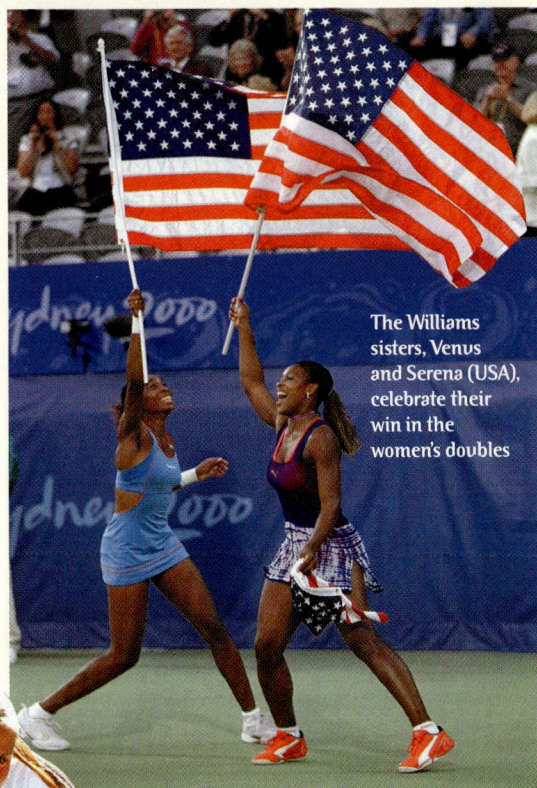

The Williams sisters, Venus and Serena (USA), celebrate their win in the women's doubles

Dokic bows out

Jelena Dokic (AUS) was Australia's big hope in the **women's singles** competition. She advanced confidently to the semifinals, her strong back court play producing sizzling winners down the sidelines. In the semifinals she came up against Elena Dementieva (RUS) and it seemed that a chance to play-off for the gold medal was looming as Dokic won the first set 6–2. But her smooth game deserted her and she made many unforced errors. The Russian held on to win 2–6, 6–4, 6–4. Dokic then went on to play Monica Seles (USA) for the bronze medal. Seles won 6–1, 6–4.

Jelena Dokic (AUS) finished fourth in the women's singles

OLYMPIC FACT

Tennis was played at the first modern Olympics in 1896, dropped in 1924 and re-introduced at the Seoul Olympic Games in 1988.

Silver swan song

The world's most decorated **men's doubles** combination, Mark Woodforde and Todd Woodbridge (AUS), left the tennis stage gracefully after winning a silver medal. The Woodies, in their last match together, were going for gold to add to their Atlanta Games success and to crown an impressive string of grand slam titles. Unfortunately for the Woodies, they were cut down by the Canadian pair of Sebastien Lareau and Daniel Nestor. The match went into a fourth set tie-break, but as if to underline that it was not to be, Woodbridge double-faulted on match point to lose 7–5, 3–6, 4–6, 6–7.

Mark Woodforde and Todd Woodbridge (AUS) end their tennis partnership with a silver medal in the men's doubles

Thrilling singles

Yevgeny Kafelnikov (RUS) went on to win gold in the men's singles

The final of the **men's singles** was an enthralling match between Yevgeny Kafelnikov (RUS) and Tommy Haas (GER) that lasted more than three-and-a-half hours. The Russian won a tie-break in the first set 7–4, after both players had broken serve twice. But Haas came out swinging in the second, and a late break allowed him to serve out the set. Now it was Kafelnikov's turn to break back, and he did so emphatically, winning the third set 6–2. But the young German would not surrender. After breaking Kafelnikov in the first game of the fourth set, he held on to tie up the match. Haas made ten unforced errors in the fifth set, and Kafelnikov took the set 6–3 to win the gold medal. The bronze medal was won by Arnaud di Pasquale (FRA).

Silver lining for Jones

In the end, it came down to a gruelling shoulder-to-shoulder sprint along Macquarie Street to the Sydney Opera House. Two athletes, one Australian and one Swiss, dug deep to find the strength to continue a battle that had started just over two hours earlier with a 1.5-kilometre swim around Farm Cove, followed by a 40-kilometre cycle leg.

Australia's Michellie Jones was the favourite to win the **women's triathlon** in its Olympic debut, but the world No. 1 knew Switzerland's Brigitte McMahon was capable of producing something special. Jones had won their World Cup clash on the same course in April 2000, but had trailed McMahon in a pre-Games race. Jones is known and feared as a tough competitor, but it was McMahon who found the strength to break clear in the run leg and sprint to the line at the steps of the Opera House. Jones secured silver, while Switzerland's Magali Messmer won the bronze.

Michellie Jones (AUS) takes silver in the women's triathlon

Canadian victory debut

A Canadian who spent several years at secondary school in Sydney, thanks to his Australian father, won the gold medal in the **men's triathlon**. Simon Whitfield, who has dual Canadian–Australian citizenship, came into the race, ranked No. 13 in the world, but was considered such an outside chance that some Canadian news organisations didn't bother to send reporters to cover the event. Whitfield was twenty-seventh after the swimming leg, and twenty-fourth after the 40-kilometre bike leg. But in a very tight race, he proved the superior runner and was delighted when he crossed the line 13.56 seconds in front of the German silver medallist, Stephan Vuckovic. Miles Stewart was the best-placed Australian in sixth place.

Simon Whitfield (CAN) crosses the line for gold

OLYMPIC FACT

The Olympic triathlon consists of a 1.5-kilometre swim in open water, a 40-kilometre bike ride and a 10-kilometre run. There is no break between stages.

See Triathlon results on page 104.

Beach Volleyball

Fun in the sun

All the fuss about the building of a stadium on Sydney's famous Bondi Beach was left behind in the staging of one of the most enjoyable and exciting events of the Games. Australians Kerri Pottharst and Natalie Cook were the stars of the show at the **women's beach volleyball**, playing some fantastic games and finishing with the gold medal.

Natalie Cook and Kerri Pottharst (AUS) were the stars of the show at the women's beach volleyball

Pottharst and Cook, bronze medallists in the inaugural event in the Atlanta Games, were an engaging pair as they worked their way through the tournament to play for gold. Twice the Australians came from behind in the final. Both sets were extremely tight contests, Australia prevailing 12–11, 12–10 against the Brazilian team of Shelda Bede and Adriana Behar. In the final set Cook served an ace to level the scores, and then a shot from Behar went wide. The Australians collapsed in the sand overcome by their win while the crowd went wild with joy.

USA dig out gold

In the **men's beach volleyball**, Brazil again had to settle for silver. Dain Blanton and Eric Fonoimoana of the USA, seeded ninth at the Sydney Olympic Games, defeated the third-seeded Brazilian team of Jose Marco Melo and Ricardo Santos in straight sets in the gold medal decider. Germany defeated Portugal in the men's bronze medal match.

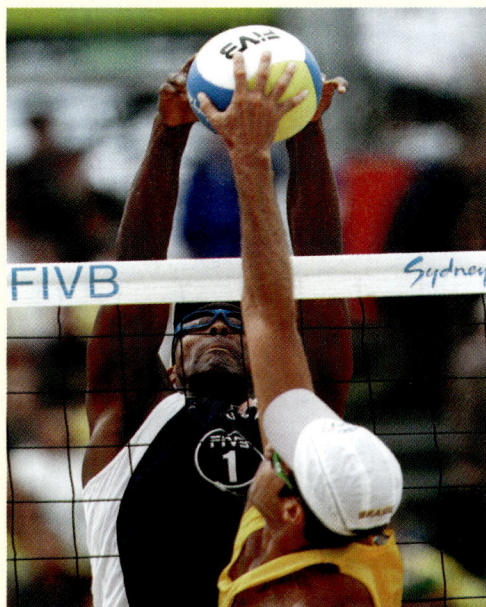

Dain Blanton (USA) blocks a Brazilian shot in the gold medal match of the men's beach volleyball

 See Beach Volleyball results on page 104.

Volleyball

Stunning victory

Italy had been a dominant force in the 1990s and went into the **men's volleyball** tournament as the hot favourite. In the end, though, they had to accept the bronze medal when Yugoslavia and the Russian Federation won their way into the play-off for gold. The first set was very close. It took a service ace from Yugoslavian star Ivan Miljkovic and a rash of Russian errors to decide it at 25–22. Yugoslavia jumped to an early lead in the second set and again won 25–22. The Russians were outplayed in the third 25–20, securing Yugoslavia the gold medal. Italy had the satisfaction of easily defeating Argentina in the bronze medal match.

A joyous victory for Yugoslavia in the men's volleyball

Decisive win

In the **women's volleyball**, Cuba won its third consecutive Olympic gold medal after a dramatic fightback against the Russian Federation. Cuba was two sets down before its giant star Regla Torres began to dominate. It closed out the best-of-five-sets match decisively, winning the last three sets 25–19, 25–18 and 15–7 (fifth sets are only played to 15 points). Brazil, the bronze medallists from the Atlanta Games, secured the same result at the Sydney Olympic Games, defeating the USA.

Regla Torres and Mireya Luis (CUB) celebrate after Cuba defeated the Russian Federation 3–2 in the gold medal match of the women's volleyball

See Volleyball results on page 104.

Weightlifting

Chinese too strong

Women's weightlifting was included for the first time on the Olympic program and China dominated the competition. The four Chinese competitors in the **women's 53 kilogram**, **women's 63 kilogram**, **women's 69 kilogram** and **women's 75+ kilogram** each won their division, while in the **women's 58 kilogram** and **women's 75 kilogram**, the gold medals went to Mexico and Colombia.

Xia Yang (CHN) on her way to winning gold in the women's 53 kilogram at the Sydney Convention Centre in Darling Harbour

The weightlifting competition had some of the gloss rubbed off in a drug crackdown. The entire Bulgarian team was expelled, but the country's 'clean' lifters were allowed back into the competition after an appeal to the Court of Arbitration of Sport. Three medallists were stripped of their medals, including Izabela Dragneva (BUL). She won the first event, the **women's 48 kilogram**, but it was handed over to Tara Nott (USA).

All eyes on Turkish stars

'The Pocket Hercules', Naim Suleymanoglu (TUR), was trying for his fourth gold medal in the **men's 62 kilogram** division. He made a bold statement by trying for an Olympic record of 145 kilograms first up, but crashed out three times to leave the field to Nikolay Pechalov (CRO), who took gold. Turkey had another hero though in the **men's 56 kilogram** division. 'The Little Dynamo', Halil Mutlu (TUR), smashed three world records on his way to a gold medal.

'The Little Dynamo', Halil Mutlu (TUR), broke three world records on his way to winning the men's 56 kilogram division

Hossein Rezazadeh (IRI) broke two world records and took gold in the **men's 105+ kilogram** over Ronny Weller (GER) and the defending champion Andrei Chemerkin (RUS), who took silver and bronze respectively. Iran took a second gold medal when Hossein Tavakoli won the **men's 105 kilogram** division. Two Greek lifters, Pyrros Dimas and Akakios Kakiasvilis both won gold medals in their class.

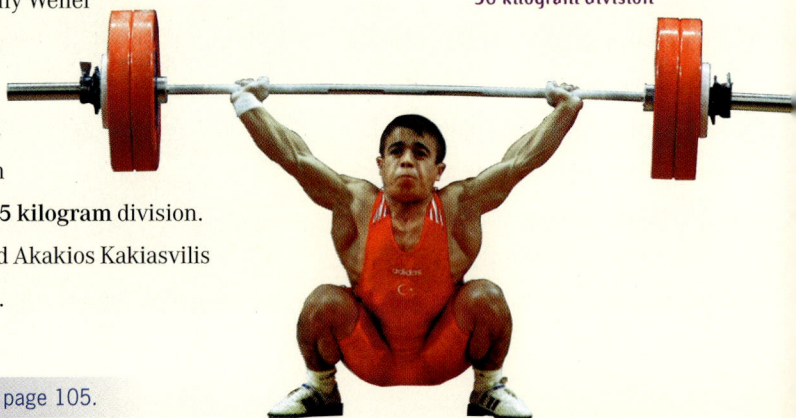

Wrestling

Freestyle

Russians pin down freestyle

The freestyle wrestlers from the Russian Federation won four gold medals of the eight decided. Russian world champion, Adam Saitiev, stunned Yoel Romero (CUB) with a furious opening in their gold medal match in the **85 kilogram** class, and held on to win gold. The **130 kilogram** final was a titanic affair, with David Moussoulbes (RUS) beating Artur Taymazov (UZB). In the **69 kilogram** division, Daniel Igali (CAN) added to his 1999 World Championship by taking gold from Arsen Gitinov (RUS). In the **76 kilogram** division Alexander Leipold (GER) won Germany's first freestyle wrestling gold medal in 40 years, defeating Brandon Slay (USA).

Alexander Leipold (GER) comes up trumps in the 76 kilogram division

Greco–Roman

Grunt for glory

The results in Sydney indicated that the dominance of Europe in Greco-Roman wrestling is waning. After the Russian Federation, the USA, Korea and Cuba all figured prominently in the medals. Gold medal wins included Kwon Ho Sim (KOR) in the **54 kilogram** division over world champion Lazaro Rivas (CUB); Filiberto Azcuy (CUB) took gold in the **69 kilogram** division. The most interest, however, centred on the **130 kilogram** contest, with Russian strongman Alexandre Kareline chasing a fourth consecutive gold medal. It was not to be, as Rulon Gardner (USA) stunned the fans, and his opponent, by inflicting the first defeat on Kareline in thirteen years.

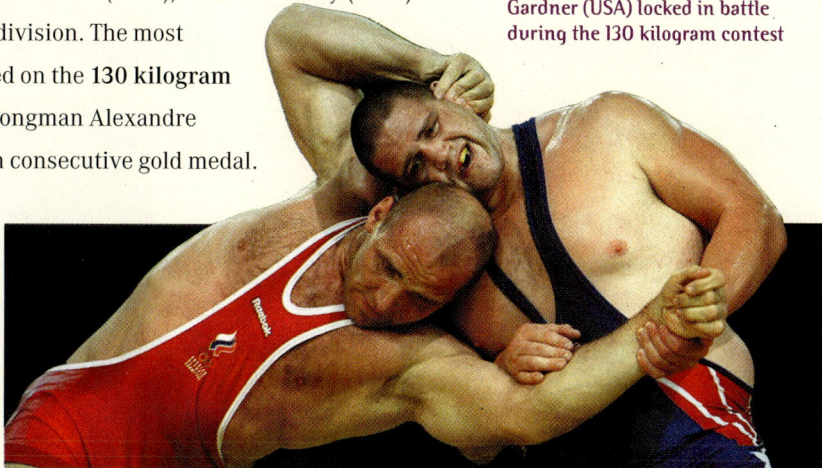

Alexandre Kareline (RUS) and Rulon Gardner (USA) locked in battle during the 130 kilogram contest

See Wrestling results on pages 105–6.

The Closing Ceremony

After 16 days of competition, the spirit of Sydney had won the hearts of people from around the world. The Closing Ceremony of the XXVII Olympiad captured the good humour, friendship and wonderful sense of fun that characterised the Sydney 2000 Games.

From the start, when a runaway ride-on lawnmower parted the marching band, flattened the podium and skittled officials, the bubble of formality was burst. The athletes entered en masse soon after, creating a ceremony that was truly about them. Leading the Australian team and carrying the national flag was multiple gold medal winner, the swimmer Ian Thorpe.

As hoped, retiring IOC president Juan Antonio Samaranch congratulated Sydney on staging 'the best Olympic Games ever'. He described the Games as 'a glorious chapter in the history of Australia' and paid tribute to 'the most dedicated and wonderful volunteers'. The Olympic flag was then passed to the next host city, Athens, for the 2004 Games. The ritual, performed with solemnity by Greek priestesses, was in stark contrast to an event that was more party than ceremony.

The Sydney 2000 Games ended with a blaze of light and colour

Olympians filled the arena

One of the highlights of the evening was the reappearance of 13-year-old Nikki Webster, this time precariously perched aloft a tall podium in front of the blazing cauldron. As the Olympic flame died, a low-flying F-111 jet lit its after-burners and carried a fiery plume across the Sydney skyline.

Into the arena came the giddy complexity of today's Australia, culminating in a parade of the icons of popular culture. There were flaming Hills Hoists on stilts, ballroom dancers performing to themes from *Strictly Ballroom*, and surreal creatures from the fruitful mind of Reg Mombasa. The band Midnight Oil performed in clothes stamped with the word 'Sorry', then Yothu Yindi continued the theme of indigenous reconciliation. Bondi Lifesavers brought in an oversized thong, bearing singer Kylie Minogue. The fin of a giant shark flipped open and out stepped golfing great Greg Norman. He was followed by children's television stars, Bananas in Pyjamas. Paul Hogan, as Crocodile Dundee, was surrounded by roller-skating crocodiles, scooter-riding buffalo and prawns on bicycles. Then came the drag queens and lavish costumes inspired by *Priscilla, Queen of the Desert*.

It was Australian to its bootstraps – some with sequins, some without. The only thing missing was Fatso the unofficial mascot, although he did feature in the Ceremony warm-up. The final song was the obvious choice – Slim Dusty led the stadium in a heart-felt 'Waltzing Matilda'.

But Sydney wouldn't be Sydney if the ceremony didn't end with an almighty bang. In what was the biggest pyrotechnic display in history, a brilliant trail of fireworks extended for 14 kilometres, from Homebush Bay, along the Parramatta River, all the way to Sydney Harbour Bridge. The Olympic Rings on the Bridge burst into flame in a finale that was simply fantastic.

The Closing Ceremony was a celebration of modern Australia, an event of tremendous flair, diversity and a touch of irreverence. It gave our 'cultural cringe' the last rites and replaced it with pride and self-confidence. While other cities will continue to stage Olympic Games, the world will never forget the Sydney 2000 Games.

Athletes danced the night away

A farewell to remember

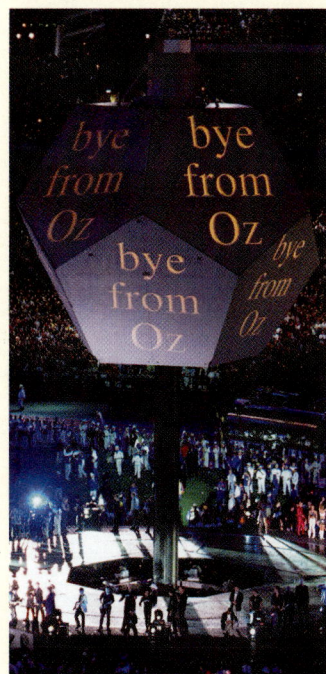

Medal tally

#	COUNTRY	G	S	B	T
1	United States of America	39	25	33	97
2	Russian Federation	32	28	28	88
3	People's Republic of China	28	16	15	59
4	**Australia**	16	25	17	58
5	Germany	14	17	26	57
6	France	13	14	11	38
7	Italy	13	8	13	34
8	Netherlands	12	9	4	25
9	Cuba	11	11	7	29
10	Great Britain	11	10	7	28
11	Romania	11	6	9	26
12	Korea	8	9	11	28
13	Hungary	8	6	3	17
14	Poland	6	5	3	14
15	Japan	5	8	5	18
16	Bulgaria	5	6	2	13
17	Greece	4	6	3	13
18	Sweden	4	5	3	12
19	Norway	4	3	3	10
20	Ethiopia	4	1	3	8
21	Ukraine	3	10	10	23
22	Kazakhstan	3	4	0	7
23	Belarus	3	3	11	17
24	Canada	3	3	8	14
25	Spain	3	3	5	11
26	Islamic Republic of Iran	3	0	1	4
26	Turkey	3	0	1	4
28	Czech Republic	2	3	3	8
29	Kenya	2	3	2	7
30	Denmark	2	3	1	6
31	Finland	2	1	1	4
32	Austria	2	1	0	3
33	Lithuania	2	0	3	5
34	Azerbaijan	2	0	1	3
35	Slovenia	2	0	0	2
36	Switzerland	1	6	2	9
37	Indonesia	1	3	2	6
38	Slovakia	1	3	1	5
39	Mexico	1	2	3	6
40	Algeria	1	1	3	5

#	COUNTRY	G	S	B	T
41	Uzbekistan	1	1	2	4
42	Latvia	1	1	1	3
42	Yugoslavia	1	1	1	3
44	Bahamas	1	1	0	2
45	New Zealand	1	0	3	4
46	Estonia	1	0	2	3
46	Thailand	1	0	2	3
48	Croatia	1	0	1	2
49	Cameroon	1	0	0	1
49	Colombia	1	0	0	1
49	Mozambique	1	0	0	1
52	Brazil	0	6	6	12
53	Jamaica	0	4	3	7
54	Nigeria	0	3	0	3
55	Belgium	0	2	3	5
55	South Africa	0	2	3	5
57	Argentina	0	2	2	4
58	Morocco	0	1	4	5
58	Chinese Taipei	0	1	4	5
60	DPR Korea	0	1	3	4
61	Saudi Arabia	0	1	1	2
61	Republic of Moldova	0	1	1	2
61	Trinidad and Tobago	0	1	1	2
64	Ireland	0	1	0	1
64	Uruguay	0	1	0	1
64	Vietnam	0	1	0	1
67	Georgia	0	0	6	6
68	Costa Rica	0	0	2	2
68	Portugal	0	0	2	2
70	Armenia	0	0	1	1
70	Barbados	0	0	1	1
70	Chile	0	0	1	1
70	India	0	0	1	1
70	Iceland	0	0	1	1
70	Israel	0	0	1	1
70	Kyrgyzstan	0	0	1	1
70	Kuwait	0	0	1	1
70	Former Yugoslav Republic of Macedonia	0	0	1	1
70	Qatar	0	0	1	1
70	Sri Lanka	0	0	1	1
	TOTAL	**301**	**299**	**328**	**928**

Australian medals

Sport	Gold	Silver	Bronze	Total
Swimming	5	9	4	18
Sailing	2	1	1	4
Cycling	1	2	3	6
Athletics	1	2	0	3
Shooting	1	1	1	3
Equestrian	1	1	0	2
Taekwondo	1	1	0	2
Hockey	1	0	1	2
Archery	1	0	0	1
Beach Volleyball	1	0	0	1
Water Polo	1	0	0	1
Rowing	0	3	2	5
Canoe/Kayak	0	1	1	2
Basketball	0	1	0	1
Gymnastics	0	1	0	1
Tennis	0	1	0	1
Triathlon	0	1	0	1
Diving	0	0	2	2
Judo	0	0	1	1
Softball	0	0	1	1
Total	**16**	**25**	**17**	**58**

Australian medal winners

Gold

To commemorate the achievements of Australia's Olympic athletes,
Australia Post produced a series of stamps featuring the gold medal winners.

Ian Thorpe – Swimming:
Men's 400 m Freestyle

Ashley Callus, Chris Fydler,
Michael Klim & Ian Thorpe –
Swimming: Men's 4 x 100 m
Freestyle Relay

Michael Diamond – Shooting:
Men's Trap

Susie O'Neill – Swimming:
Women's 200 m Freestyle

William Kirby, Michael Klim,
Todd Pearson & Ian Thorpe –
Swimming: Men's 4 x 200 m
Freestyle Relay

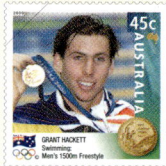

Grant Hackett – Swimming:
Men's 1500 m Freestyle

Simon Fairweather – Archery:
Men's Individual

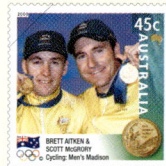

Brett Aitken & Scott McGrory –
Cycling: Men's Madison

Lauren Burns – Taekwondo:
Women's Under 49 kg

Jenny Armstrong & Belinda
Stowell – Sailing: Women's 470

Tom King & Mark Turnbull –
Sailing: Men's 470

Phillip Dutton, Andrew Hoy,
Matt Ryan & Stuart Tinney –
Equestrian: Team Three Day
Event

Naomi Castle, Joanne Fox,
Bridgette Gusterson, Simone
Hankin, Yvette Higgins, Kate
Hooper, Bronwyn Mayer, Gail
Miller, Melissa Mills, Debbie
Watson, Liz Weekes, Danielle
Woodhouse, Taryn Woods –
Women's Water Polo

Katie Allen, Alyson Annan, Lisa
Carruthers, Renita Garard, Juliet
Haslam, Rechelle Hawkes,
Nikki Hudson, Rachel Imison,
Clover Maitland, Claire Mitchell-
Taverner, Jenny Morris, Alison
Peek, Katrina Powell, Angie
Skirving, Kate Starre, Julie
Towers – Women's Hockey

Natalie Cook & Kerri Pottharst –
Women's Beach Volleyball

Cathy Freeman – Athletics:
Women's 400 m

Silver and bronze

AQUATICS

Diving
Men
3 m Springboard Synchronized
Bronze – Robert Newberry & Dean Pullar
Women
10 m Platform Synchronized
Bronze – Rebecca Gilmore & Loudy Tourky

Swimming
Men
100 m Backstroke
Silver – Matt Welsh
Men
200 m Backstroke
Bronze – Matt Welsh
Men
100 m Butterfly
Silver – Michael Klim
Bronze – Geoff Huegill
Men
200 m Butterfly
Bronze – Justin Norris
Men
200 m Freestyle
Silver – Ian Thorpe
Men
1500 m Freestyle
Silver – Kieren Perkins
Men
4 x 100 m Team Medley
Silver – Regan Harrison, Geoff Huegill, Michael Klim & Matt Welsh
Women
100 m Breaststroke
Silver – Leisel Jones
Women
200 m Butterfly
Silver – Susie O'Neill
Bronze – Petria Thomas
Women
4 x 200 m Freestyle Relay
Silver – Susie O'Neill, Giaan Rooney, Petria Thomas & Kirsten Thomson
Women
4 x 100 m Team Medley

Silver – Dyana Calub, Leisel Jones, Susie O'Neill & Petria Thomas

ATHLETICS

Field
Men
Long Jump
Silver – Jai Taurima
Women
Pole Vault
Silver – Tatiana Grigorieva

BASKETBALL
Women
Silver – Carla Boyd, Sandy Brondello, Trish Fallon, Michelle Griffiths, Kristi Harrower, Jo Hill, Lauren Jackson, Annie la Fleur, Shelley Sandie, Rachael Sporn, Michele Timms & Jenny Whittle

CANOE/KAYAK

Sprint (Kayak)
Men
K2 500 m
Silver – Daniel Collins & Andrew Trim
Women
K1 500 m
Bronze – Katrin Borchert

CYCLING

Track
Men
Individual Pursuit
Bronze – Brad McGee
Men
1 km Time Trial
Bronze – Shane Kelly
Men
Keirin
Silver – Gary Neiwand
Men
Olympic Sprint
Bronze – Sean Eadie, Darryn Hill & Gary Neiwand

Women
500 m Time Trial
Silver – Michelle Ferris

EQUESTRIAN

Three Day Event
Individual
Silver – Andrew Hoy

GYMNASTICS

Trampoline
Men
Silver – Ji Wallace

HOCKEY
Men
Bronze – Michael Brennan, Adam Commens, Stephen Davies, Damon Diletti, Lachlan Dreher, Jason Duff, Troy Elder, James Elmer, Paul Gaudoin, Stephen Holt, Brent Livermore, Daniel Sproule, Jay Stacy, Craig Victory, Matthew Wells & Michael York

JUDO
Women
57 kg
Bronze – Maria Pekli

ROWING
Men
Coxless Pair
Bronze – Matthew Long & James Tomkins
Men
Coxless Four
Bronze – Ben Dodwell, Bo Hanson, Geoff Stewart & James Stewart
Men
Lightweight Coxless Four
Silver – Darren Balmforth, Simon Burgess, Anthony Edwards & Robert Richards
Men
Eight

Silver – Daniel Burke, Jaime Fernandez, Alastair Gordon, Brett Hayman, Robert Jahrling, Mike McKay, Nick Porzig, Christian Ryan & Stuart Welch
Women
Coxless Pair
Silver – Kate Slatter & Rachel Taylor

SAILING
Open
Laser
Bronze – Michael Blackburn
Open
Tornado
Silver – Darren Bundock & John Forbes

SHOOTING
Men
Double Trap
Silver – Russell Mark
Women
10 m Air Pistol
Bronze – Annemarie Forder

SOFTBALL
Women
Bronze – Sandra Allen, Joanne Brown, Kerry Dienelt, Peta Edebone, Sue Fairhurst, Selina Follas, Fiona Hanes, Kelly Hardie, Tanya Harding, Sally McCreedy, Simmone Morrow, Melanie Roche, Natalie Titcume, Natalie Ward & Brooke Wilkins

TAEKWONDO
Men
80+ kg
Silver – Daniel Trenton

TENNIS
Men
Doubles
Silver – Todd Woodbridge & Mark Woodforde

TRIATHLON
Women
Silver – Michellie Jones

Results: Sydney 2000 Olympic Games

Note: See page 107 for nation abbreviations.

Aquatics   Diving, Swimming, Synchronized Swimming, Water Polo

Diving

Event	1996 Gold Medal Winner	Bronze	Silver	Gold (pts)
Men				
3 m Springboard	Xiong Ni (CHN)	Dmitri Saoutine (RUS)	Fernando Platas (MEX)	Xiong Ni (CHN) 708.72
10 m Platform	Dmitri Sautin (RUS)	Dmitri Saoutine (RUS)	Hu Jia (CHN)	Tian Liang (CHN) 724.53
3 m Springboard synchronized	New event	Australia	Russian Federation	People's Republic of China 365.58
10 m Platform synchronized	New event	Germany	People's Republic of China	Russia 365.04
Women				
3 m Springboard	Fu Mingxia (CHN)	Doerte Lindner (GER)	Guo Jingjing (CHN)	Fu Mingxia (CHN) 609.42
10 m Platform	Fu Mingxia (CHN)	Anne Montminy (CAN)	Li Na (CHN)	Laura Wilkinson (USA) 543.75
3 m Springboard synchronized	New event	Ukraine	People's Republic of China	Russian Federation 332.64
10 m Platform synchronized	New event	Australia	Canada	People's Republic of China 345.12

Swimming

Current Records as at 01/10/2000

Event	World Record (min)	Olympic Record (min)	Bronze	Silver	Gold (min)	WR/OR
Men						
Backstroke						
100 m	Lenny Krayzelburg (USA) 0:53.60	Lenny Krayzelburg (USA) 0:53.72	Stev Theloke (GER)	Matthew Welsh (AUS)	Lenny Krayzelburg (USA) 0:53.72	OR
200 m	Lenny Krayzelburg (USA) 1:55.87	Lenny Krayzelburg (USA) 1:56.76	Matthew Welsh (AUS)	Aaron Peirsol (USA)	Lenny Krayzelburg (USA) 1:56.76	OR

New Record

Swimming (cont'd)

Current Records as at 01/10/2000

Event	World Record (min)	Olympic Record (min)	Bronze	Silver	Gold (min)	New Record WR/OR
Breaststroke						
100 m	Roman Sludnov (RUS) 1:00.36	Domenico Fioravanti (ITA) 1:00.46	Roman Sludnov (RUS)	Ed Moses (USA)	Domenico Fioravanti (ITA) 1:00.46	OR
200 m	Mike Barrowman (USA) 2:10.16	Mike Barrowman (USA) 2:10.16	Davide Rummolo (ITA)	Terence Parkin (RSA)	Domenico Fioravanti (ITA) 2:10.87	
Butterfly						
100 m	Michael Klim (AUS) 0:51.81	Geoff Huegill (AUS) 0:51.96	Geoff Huegill (AUS)	Michael Klim (AUS)	Lars Froelander (SWE) 0:52.00	
200 m	Tom Malchow (USA) 1:55.18	Tom Malchow (USA) 1:55.35	Justin Norris (AUS)	Denys Sylant'yev (UKR)	Tom Malchow (USA) 1:55.35	OR
Freestyle						
50 m	Alexander Popov (RUS) 21.64	Alexander Popov (RUS) 0:21.91	Pieter van den Hoogenband (NED)		Anthony Ervin & Gary Hall Jr (USA) 0:21.98	
100 m	Pieter van den Hoogenband (NED) 0:47.84	Pieter van den Hoogenband (NED) 0:47.84	Gary Hall Jr (USA)	Alexander Popov (RUS)	Pieter van den Hoogenband (NED) 0:48.30	
200 m	Pieter van den Hoogenband (NED) 1:45.35	Pieter van den Hoogenband (NED) 1:45.35	Massimiliano Rosolino (ITA)	Ian Thorpe (AUS)	Pieter van den Hoogenband (NED) 1:45.35	WR OR
400 m	Ian Thorpe (AUS) 3:40.59	Ian Thorpe (AUS) 3:40.59	Klete Keller (USA)	Massimiliano Rosolino (ITA)	Ian Thorpe (AUS) 3:40.59	WR OR
1500 m	Kieren Perkins (AUS) 14:41.66	Kieren Perkins (AUS) 14:43.48	Chris Thompson (USA)	Kieren Perkins (AUS)	Grant Hackett (AUS) 14:48.33	
4 x 100 m	Australia 3:13.67	Australia 3:13.67	Brazil	United States of America	Australia 3:13.67	WR OR
4 x 200 m	Australia 7:07.05	Australia 7:07.05	Netherlands	United States of America	Australia 7:07.05	WR OR
Individual medley						
200 m	Jani Sievinen (FIN) 1:58.16	Massimiliano Rosolino (ITA) 1:58.98	Tom Wilkens (USA)	Tom Dolan (USA)	Massimiliano Rosolino (ITA) 1:58.98	OR
400 m	Tom Dolan (USA) 4:11.76	Tom Dolan (USA) 4:11.76	Curtis Myden (CAN)	Erik Vendt (USA)	Tom Dolan (USA) 4:11.76	WR OR
Team medley						
4 x 100 m	United States of America 3:33.73	United States of America 3:33.73	Germany	Australia	United States of America 3:33.73	WR OR
Women						
Backstroke						
100 m	He Cihong (CHN) 1:00.16	Diana Mocanu (ROM) 1:00.21	Nina Zhivanevskaya (ESP)	Mai Nakamura (JPN)	Diana Mocanu (ROM) 1:00.21	OR
200 m	Krisztina Egerszegi (HUN) 2:06.62	Krisztina Egerszegi (HUN) 2:07.06	Miki Nakao (JPN)	Roxana Maracineanu (FRA)	Diana Mocanu (ROM) 2:08.16	
Breaststroke						
100 m	Penelope Heyns (RSA) 1:06.52	Penelope Heyns (RSA) 1:07.02	Penelope Heyns (RSA)	Leisel Jones (AUS)	Megan Quann (USA) 1:07.05	
200 m	Penelope Heyns (RSA) 2:23.64	Agnes Kovacs (HUN) 2:24.35	Amanda Beard (USA)	Kristy Kowal (USA)	Agnes Kovacs (HUN) 2:24.35	OR
Butterfly						
100 m	Inge de Bruijn (NED) 0:56.61	Inge de Bruijn (NED) 0:56.61	Dara Torres (USA)	Martina Moravcova (SVK)	Inge de Bruijn (NED) 0:56.61	WR OR
200 m	Susie O'Neill (AUS) 2:05.81	Misty Hyman (USA) 2:05.88	Petria Thomas (AUS)	Susie O'Neill (AUS)	Misty Hyman (USA) 2:05.88	OR
Freestyle						
50 m	Inge de Bruijn (NED) 0:24.13	Inge de Bruijn (NED) 0:24.13	Dara Torres (USA)	Therese Alshammar (SWE)	Inge de Bruijn (NED) 0:24.32	
100 m	Inge de Bruijn (NED) 0:53.77	Inge de Bruijn (NED) 0:53.77	Jenny Thompson & Dara Torres (USA)	Therese Alshammar (SWE)	Inge de Bruijn (NED) 0:53.83	
200 m	Franziska van Almsick (GER) 1:56.78	Heike Friedrich (GDR) 1:57.65	Claudia Poll (CRC)	Martina Moravcova (SVK)	Susie O'Neill (AUS) 1:58.24	
400 m	Janet Evans (USA) 4:03.85	Janet Evans (USA) 4:03.85	Claudia Poll (CRC)	Diana Munz (USA)	Brooke Bennett (USA) 4:05.80	
800 m	Janet Evans (USA) 8:16.22	Brooke Bennett (USA) 8:19.67	Kaitlin Sandeno (USA)	Yana Klochkova (UKR)	Brooke Bennett (USA) 8:19.67	OR
4 x 100 m	United States of America 3:36.61	United States of America 3:36.61	Sweden	Netherlands	United States of America 3:36.61	WR OR
4 x 200 m	East Germany 7:55.47	United States of America 7:57.80	Germany	Australia	United States of America 7:57.80	OR

Swimming (cont'd)

Current Records as at 01/10/2000

Event	World Record (min)	Olympic Record (min)	Bronze	Silver	Gold (min)	New Record WR/OR
Women						
Individual medley						
200 m	Wu Yanyan (CHN) 2:09.72	Yana Klochkova (UKR) 2:10.68	Cristina Teuscher (USA)	Beatrice Caslaru (ROM)	Yana Klochkova (UKR) 2:10.68	OR
400 m	Yana Klochkova (UKR) 4:33.59	Yana Klochkova (UKR) 4:33.59	Beatrice Caslaru (ROM)	Yasuko Tajima (JPN)	Yana Klochkova (UKR) 4:33.59	WR OR
Team medley						
4 x 100 m	United States of America 3:58.30	United States of America 3:58.30	Japan	Australia	United States of America 3:58.30	WR OR

Synchronized Swimming

Event	1996 Gold Medal Winner	Bronze	Silver	Gold (pts)
Duet	New event	France	Japan	Russian Federation 99.580
Team	United States of America	Canada	Japan	Russian Federation 99.146

Water Polo

Event	1996 Gold Medal Winner	Bronze	Silver	Gold
Men				
	Spain	Yugoslavia	Russian Federation	Hungary
Women				
	New event	Russian Federation	United States of America	Australia

Archery

Current Records as at 01/10/2000

Event	World Record (pts)	Olympic Record (pts)	Bronze	Silver	Gold (pts)	New Record WR/OR
Men						
Individual	Kyung-Mo Park (KOR) 119	Kyo-Moon Oh (KOR) 115	Wietse van Alten (NED)	Victor Wunderle (USA)	Simon Fairweather (AUS) 113	
Team	Korea 260	Korea 258	United States of America	Italy	Korea 255	
Women						
Individual	Hyo-Jung Kim (KOR) 117	Soo-Nyung Kim (KOR) 114	Soo-Nyung Kim (KOR)	Nam-Soon Kim (KOR)	Mi-Jin Yun (KOR) 107	
Team	Korea 253	Korea 249	Germany	Ukraine	Korea 251	

Current Records as at 01/10/2000

New Record

Event	World Record	Olympic Record	Bronze	Silver	Gold	WR/OR
Men						
100 m	Maurice Greene (USA) 0:09.79 min	Donovan Bailey (CAN) 0:09.84 min	Obadele Thompson (BAR)	Ato Boldon (TRI)	Maurice Greene (USA) 0:09.87 min	
200 m	Michael Johnson (USA) 0:19.32 min	Michael Johnson (USA) 0:19.32 min	Ato Boldon (TRI)	Darren Campbell (GBR)	Konstantinos Kenteris (GRE) 0:20.09 min	
400 m	Michael Johnson (USA) 0:43.18 min	Michael Johnson (USA) 0:43.49 min	Gregory Haughton (JAM)	Alvin Harrison (USA)	Michael Johnson (USA) 0:43.84 min	
800 m	Wilson Kipketer (DEN) 1:41.11 min	Vebjørn Rodahl (NOR) 1:42.58 min	Aissa Djabir Saïd-Guerni (ALG)	Wilson Kipketer (DEN)	Nils Schumann (GER) 1:45.08 min	
1500 m	Hicham El Guerrouj (MAR) 3:26.00 min	Noah Ngeny (KEN) 3:32.07 min	Bernard Lagat (KEN)	Hicham El Guerrouj (MAR)	Noah Ngeny (KEN) 3:32.07 min	OR
5000 m	Haile Gebrselassie (ETH) 12:39.36 min	Saïd Aouita (MAR) 13:05.59 min	Brahim Lahlafi (MAR)	Ali Saïdi-Sief (ALG)	Millon Wolde (ETH) 13:35.49 min	
10 000 m	Haile Gebrselassie (ETH) 26:22.75 min	Haile Gebrselassie (ETH) 27:07.34 min	Assefa Mezgebu (ETH)	Paul Tergat (KEN)	Haile Gebrselassie (ETH) 27:18.20 min	
20 km Walk	Julio Martínez (GUA) & Roman Rasskazov (RUS) 1:17:46 min*	Robert Korzeniowski (POL) 1:18:59 min*	Vladimir Andreyev (RUS)	Noe Hernandez (MEX)	Robert Korzeniowski (POL) 1:18:59 min	
50 km Walk	Valeriy Spitsyn (RUS) 3:37:26 min*	Vyacheslav Ivanenko (URS) 3:38:29 min*	Joel Sanchez (MEX)	Aigars Fadejevs (LAT)	Robert Korzeniowski (POL) 3:42:22 min	
3000 m Steeplechase	Bernard Barmasai (KEN) 7:55.72 min	Julius Kariuki (KEN) 8:05.51 min	Ali Ezzine (MAR)	Wilson Boit Kipketer (KEN)	Reuben Kosgei (KEN) 8:21.43 min	
Marathon	Khalid Khannouchi (MAR) 2:05:42 min*	Carlos Lopes (POR) 2:09:21 min*	Tesfaye Tola (ETH)	Eric Wainaina (KEN)	Gezahgne Abera (ETH) 2:10:11 min	
110 m Hurdles	Colin Jackson (GBR) 0:12.91 min	Allen Johnson (USA) 0:12.95 min	Mark Crear (USA)	Terrence Trammell (USA)	Anier Garcia (CUB) 0:13.00 min	
400 m Hurdles	Kevin Young (USA) 0:46.78 min	Kevin Young (USA) 0:46.78 min	Llewellyn Herbert (RSA)	Hadi Souan Somayli (KSA)	Angelo Taylor (USA) 0:47.50 min	
High jump	Javier Sotomayor (CUB) 2.45 m	Charles Austin (USA) 2.39 m	Abderrahmane Hammad (ALG)	Javier Sotomayor (CUB)	Sergey Klugin (RUS) 2.35 m	
Long jump	Mike Powell (USA) 8.95 m	Bob Beamon (USA) 8.90 m	Roman Schurenko (UKR)	Jai Taurima (AUS)	Ivan Pedroso (CUB) 8.55 m	
Triple jump	Jonathan Edwards (GBR) 18.29 m	Kenny Harrison (USA) 18.09 m	Denis Kapustin (RUS)	Yoel Garcia (CUB)	Jonathan Edwards (GBR) 17.71 m	
Pole vault	Sergey Bubka (UKR) 6.14 m	Jean Galfione (FRA), Andrei Tivontschik (GER) & Igor Trandenkov (RUS) 5.92 m	Maksim Tarasov (RUS)	Lawrence Johnson (USA)	Nick Hysong (USA) 5.90 m	
Shot put	Randy Barnes (USA) 23.12 m	Ulf Timmermann (GDR) 22.47 m	John Godina (USA)	Adam Nelson (USA)	Arsi Harju (FIN) 21.29 m	
Javelin	Ján Zelezny (CZE) 98.48 m	Ján Zelezny (CZE) 90.17 m	Sergey Makarov (RUS)	Steve Backley (GBR)	Ján Zelezny (CZE) 90.17 m	OR
Discus	Jürgen Schult (GDR) 74.08 m	Lars Riedel (GER) 69.40 m	Frantz Kruger (RSA)	Lars Riedel (GER)	Virgilijus Alekna (LTU) 69.30 m	
Hammer	Yuriy Sedykh (URS) 86.74 m	Sergey Litvinov (URS) 84.80 m	Igor Astapkovich (BLR)	Nicola Vizzoni (ITA)	Szymon Ziolkowski (POL) 80.02 m	
Relay						
4 x 100 m	United States of America 0:37.40 min	United States of America 0:37.40 min	Cuba	Brazil	United States of America 0:37.61 min	
4 x 400 m	United States of America 2:54.20 min	United States of America 2:55.74 min	Jamaica	Nigeria	United States of America 2:56.35 min	
Decathlon	Tomáš Dvořák (CZE) 8994 pts	Daley Thompson (GBR) 8847 pts	Chris Huffins (USA)	Roman Sebrle (CZE)	Erki Nool (EST) 8641 pts	
Women						
100 m	Florence Griffith Joyner (USA) 0:10.49 min	Florence Griffith Joyner (USA) 0:10.62 min	Tanya Lawrence (JAM)	Ekaterini Thanou (GRE)	Marion Jones (USA) 0:10.75 min	
200 m	Florence Griffith Joyner (USA) 0:21.34 min	Florence Griffith Joyner (USA) 0:21.34 min	Susanthika Jayasinghe (SRI)	Pauline Davis-Thompson (BAH)	Marion Jones (USA) 0:21.84 min	
400 m	Marita Koch (GDR) 0:47.60 min	Marie-José Pérec (FRA) 0:48.25 min	Katharine Merry (GBR)	Lorraine Graham (JAM)	Cathy Freeman (AUS) 0:49.11 min	
800 m	Jarmila Kratochvílová (TCH) 1:53.28 min	Nadezhda Olizarenko (URS) 1:53.43 min	Kelly Holmes (GBR)	Stephanie Graf (AUT)	Maria Mutola (MOZ) 1:56.15 min	

Athletics (cont'd)

Current Records as at 01/10/2000

Event	World Record	Olympic Record	Bronze	Silver	Gold	WR/OR	New Record
Women							
1500 m	Qu Yunxia (CHN) 3:50.46 min	Paula Ivan (ROM) 3:53.96 min	Gabriela Szabo (ROM)	Violeta Szekely (ROM)	Nouria Merah-Benida (ALG) 4:05.10 min		
5000 m	Jiang Bo (CHN) 14:28.09 min	Gabriela Szabo (ROM) 14:40.79 min	Gete Wami (ETH)	Sonia O'Sullivan (IRL)	Gabriela Szabo (ROM) 14:40.79 min		OR
10 000 m	Wang Yunxia (CHN) 29:31.78 min	Derartu Tulu (ETH) 30:17.49 min	Fernanda Ribeiro (POR)	Gete Wami (ETH)	Derartu Tulu (ETH) 30:17.49 min		OR
20 km Walk	Tatyana Gudkova (CHN) 1:25:18 min*	Wang Liping (CHN) 1:29:05 min*	Maria Vasco (ESP)	Kjersti Plaetzer (NOR)	Wang Liping (CHN) 1:29:05 min		OR
Marathon	Tegla Loroupe (KEN) 2:20:43 min*	Naoko Takahashi (JPN) 2:23:14 min*	Joyce Chepchumba (KEN)	Lidia Simon (ROM)	Naoko Takahashi (JPN) 2:23:14 min		OR
100 m Hurdles	Yordanka Donkova (BUL) 0:12.21 min	Yordanka Donkova (BUL) 0:12.38 min	Melissa Morrison (USA)	Glory Alozie (NGR)	Olga Shishigina (KAZ) 0:12.65 min		
400 m Hurdles	Kim Batten (USA) 0:52.61 min	Deon Hemmings (JAM) 0:52.82 min	Nouzha Bidouane (MAR)	Deon Hemmings (JAM)	Irina Privalova (RUS) 0:53.02 min		
High jump	Stefka Kostadinova (BUL) 2.09 m	Stefka Kostadinova (BUL) 2.05 m	Kajsa Bergqvist (SWE)	Hestrie Cloete (RSA)	Yelena Yelesina (RUS) 2.01 m		
Long jump	Galina Chistyakova (URS) 7.52 m	Jackie Joyner-Kersee (USA) 7.40 m	Marion Jones (USA)	Fiona May (ITA)	Heike Drechsler (GER) 6.99 m		
Triple jump	Inessa Kravets (UKR) 15.50 m	Inessa Kravets (UKR) 15.33 m	Olena Hovorova (UKR)	Tatyana Lebedeva (RUS)	Tereza Marinova (BUL) 15.20 m		OR
Pole vault	Stacy Dragila (USA) 4.63 m	Stacy Dragila (USA) 4.60 m	Vala Flosadottir (ISL)	Tatiana Grigorieva (AUS)	Stacy Dragila (USA) 4.60 m		OR
Shot put	Natalya Lisovskaya (URS) 22.63 m	Ilona Slupianek (GDR) 22.41 m	Astrid Kumbernuss (GER)	Larisa Peleshenko (RUS)	Yanina Korolchik (BLR) 20.56 m		
Javelin	Trine Hattestad (NOR) 69.48 m	Trine Hattestad (NOR) 68.91 m	Osleidys Menendez (CUB)	Mirella Maniani-Tzelili (GRE)	Trine Hattestad (NOR) 68.91 m		OR
Discus	Gaby Reinsch (GDR) 76.80 m	Martina Hellmann (GDR) 72.30 m	Irina Yatchenko (BLR)	Ellina Zvereva (BLR)	Ellina Zvereva (BLR) 68.40 m		
Hammer	Mihaela Melinte (ROM) 76.07 m	Kamila Skolimowska (POL) 71.16 m	Kirsten Muenchow (GER)	Olga Kuzenkova (RUS)	Kamila Skolimowska (POL) 71.16 m		OR
Relay							
4 x 100 m	East Germany 0:41.37 min	East Germany 0:41.60 min	United States of America	Bahamas	Bahamas 0:41.95 min		
4 x 400 m	Soviet Union 3:15.17 min	Soviet Union 3:15.17 min	Russian Federation	United States of America	United States of America 3:22.62 min		
Heptathlon	Jackie Joyner-Kersee (USA) 7291 pts	Jackie Joyner-Kersee (USA) 7291 pts	Natalya Sazanovich (BLR)	Yelena Prokhorova (RUS)	Denise Lewis (GBR) 6584 pts		

*This event is contested on courses that vary each year. As such, this time is not recognised by the IAAF as a record and therefore must be considered as a World/Olympic Best Performance.

Badminton

Event	1996 Gold Medal Winner	Bronze	Silver	Gold
Men				
Singles	Poul-Erik Hoyer-Larsen (DEN)	Xia Xuanze (CHN)	Hendrawan (INA)	Ji Xinpeng (CHN)
Doubles	Indonesia	Korea	Korea	Indonesia
Women				
Singles	Bang Soo-Hyun (KOR)	Ye Zhaoying (CHN)	Camilla Martin (DEN)	Gong Zhichao (CHN)
Doubles	China	People's Republic of China	People's Republic of China	People's Republic of China
Open				
Mixed Doubles	Korea	Great Britain	Indonesia	People's Republic of China

Baseball

Event	1996 Gold Medal Winner	Bronze	Silver	Gold
Men	Cuba	Korea	Cuba	United States of America

Basketball

Event	1996 Gold Medal Winner	Bronze	Silver	Gold
Men	United States of America	Lithuania	France	United States of America
Women	United States of America	Brazil	Australia	United States of America

Boxing

Event	1996 Gold Medal Winner	Bronze	Silver	Gold
Light flyweight 48 kg	Daniel Petrov (BUL)	Un Chol Kim (PRK) & Maikro Romero Esquirol (CUB)	Rafael Lozano Munoz (ESP)	Brahim Asloum (FRA)
Flyweight 51 kg	Maikro Romero (CUB)	Jerome Thomas (FRA) & Vladimir Sidorenko (UKR)	Bulat Jumadilov (KAZ)	Wijan Ponlid (THA)
Bantamweight 54 kg	Istvan Kovacs (HUN)	Serguey Daniltchenko (UKR) & Clarence Vinson (USA)	Raimkoul Malakhbekov (RUS)	Guillermo Rigondeaux Ortiz (CUB)
Featherweight 57 kg	Sornluck Kamsing (THA)	Tahar Tamsamani (MAR) & Kamil Dzamalutdinov (RUS)	Ricardo Juarez (USA)	Bekzat Sattarkhanov (KAZ)
Lightweight 60 kg	Hocine Soltani (ALG)	Cristian Bejarano Benitez (MEX) & Alexandr Maletin (RUS)	Andriy Kotelnyk (UKR)	Mario Kindelan (CUB)
Light welterweight 63.5 kg	Hector Vinent (CUB)	Mohamed Allalou (ALG) & Diogenes Luna Martinez (CUB)	Ricardo Williams (USA)	Mahamadkadyz Abdullaev (UZB)
Welterweight 67 kg	Oleg Saitov (RUS)	Vitali Grusac (MDA) & Dorel Simion (ROM)	Sergey Dotsenko (UKR)	Oleg Saitov (RUS)
Light middleweight 71 kg	David Reid (USA)	Jermain Taylor (USA) & Porchai Thongburan (THA)	Marin Simion (ROM)	Yermakhan Ibraimov (KAZ)
Middleweight 75 kg	Ariel Hernandez (CUB)	Vugar Alekperov (AZE) & Zsolt Erdei (HUN)	Gaidarbek Gaidarbekov (RUS)	Jorge Gutierrez (CUB)
Light heavyweight 81 kg	Vasili Jirov (KAZ)	Andri Fedtchouk (UKR) & Sergei Mikhailov (UZB)	Rudolf Kraj (CZE)	Alexander Lebziak (RUS)

Boxing (cont'd)

Event	1996 Gold Medal Winner	Silver	Bronze	Gold
Heavyweight 91 kg	Felix Savon (CUB)	Sultanahmed Ibzagimov (RUS)	Sebastian Kober (GER) & Vladimir Tchantouria (GEO)	Felix Savon (CUB)
Super heavyweight 91+ kg	Vladimir Klichko (UKR)	Mukhtarkhan Dildabekov (KAZ)	Rustam Saidov (UZB) & Paolo Vidoz (ITA)	Audley Harrison (GBR)

Canoe/Kayak Slalom, Sprint

Slalom

Canoe

Event	1996 Gold Medal Winner	Silver	Bronze	Gold (pts)
Men				
C1	Michal Martikan (SVK)	Michal Martikan (SVK)	Juraj Mincik (SVK)	Tony Estanguet (FRA) 115.25
C2	France	Poland	Czech Republic	Slovakia 237.74

Kayak

Event	1996 Gold Medal Winner	Silver	Bronze	Gold (pts)
Men				
K1	Oliver Fix (GER)	Paul Ratcliffe (GBR)	Pierpaolo Ferrazzi (ITA)	Thomas Schmidt (GER) 217.25
Women				
K1	Stepanka Hilgertova (CZE)	Brigitte Guibal (FRA)	Anne-Lise Bardet (FRA)	Stepanka Hilgertova (CZE) 125.21

Sprint

Canoe

Event	1996 Gold Medal Winner	Silver	Bronze	Gold (min)
Men				
C1 500 m	Martin Doktor (CZE)	Maxim Opalev (RUS)	Andreas Dittmer (GER)	Gyorgy Kolonics (HUN) 2:24.813
C1 1000 m	Martin Dokter (CZE)	Ledys Frank Balceiro (CUB)	Steve Giles (CAN)	Andreas Dittmer (GER) 3:54.379
C2 500 m	Hungary	Poland	Romania	Hungary 1:51.284
C2 1000 m	Germany	Cuba	Germany	Romania 3:37.355

Canoe/Kayak (cont'd)

Kayak

Event	1996 Gold Medal Winner	Bronze	Silver	Gold (min)
Men				
K1 500 m	Antonio Rossi (ITA)	Michael Kolganov (ISR)	Petar Merkov (BUL)	Knut Holmann (NOR) 1:57.847
K1 1000 m	Knut Holmann (NOR)	Tim Brabants (GBR)	Petar Merkov (BUL)	Knut Holmann (NOR) 3:33.269
K2 500 m	Germany	Germany	Australia	Hungary 1:47.055
K2 1000 m	Italy	Hungary	Sweden	Italy 3:14.461
K4 1000 m	Germany	Poland	Germany	Hungary 2:55.188
Women				
K1 500 m	Rita Koban (HUN)	Australia	Canada	Italy 2:13.848
K2 500 m	Sweden	Poland	Hungary	Germany 1:56.996
K4 500 m	Germany	Romania	Hungary	Germany 1:34.532

Cycling Mountain bike, Road, Track

Mountain Bike

Event	1996 Gold Medal Winner	Bronze	Silver	Gold (min)
Men				
	Bart Brentjens (NED)	Christoph Sauser (SUI)	Filip Meirhaeghe (BEL)	Miguel Martinez (FRA) 2:09:02.50
Women				
	Paola Pezzo (ITA)	Margarita Fullana (ESP)	Barbara Blatter (SUI)	Paola Pezzo (ITA) 1:49:24.38

Road

Event	1996 Gold Medal Winner	Bronze	Silver	Gold (min)
Men				
Road race	Pascal Richard (SUI)	Andreas Kloeden (GER)	Alexandre Vinokourov (KAZ)	Jan Ullrich (GER) 5:29:08.00
Time trial	Miguel Indurain (ESP)	Lance Armstrong (USA)	Jan Ullrich (GER)	Viacheslav Ekimov (RUS) 57:40.00
Women				
Road race	Jeannie Longo-Ciprelli (FRA)	Diana Ziliute (LTU)	Hanka Kupfernagel (GER)	Leontien Zijlaard (NED) 3:06:31.00
Time trial	Zulfia Zabirova (RUS)	Jeannie Longo-Ciprelli (FRA)	Mari Holden (USA)	Leontien Zijlaard (NED) 42:00.00

Cycling (cont'd)

Track

| | Current Records as at 01/10/2000 | | | | | New Record |
Event	World Record (min)	Olympic Record (min)	Bronze	Silver	Gold	WR/OR
Men						
Individual pursuit	Chris Boardman (GBR) 4:11.114	Robert Bartko (GER) 4:18.515	Brad McGee (AUS)	Jens Lehmann (GER)	Robert Bartko (GER) 4:18.515 min	OR
1 km Time trial	Arnaud Tournant (FRA) 1:00.148	Jason Queally (GER) 1:01.609	Shane Kelly (AUS)	Stefan Nimke (GER)	Jason Queally (GER) 1:01.609 min	OR
1 km Points race	N/A	N/A	Alexey Markov (RUS)	Milton Wynants (URU)	Juan Llaneras (ESP) 14 pts	
Madison	N/A	N/A	Italy	Belgium	Australia 26 pts	
Team pursuit	Germany 3:59.710	Germany 3:59.710	Great Britain	Ukraine	Germany 3:59.710 min	WR OR
Keirin	N/A	N/A	Jens Fiedler (GER)	Gary Neiwand (AUS)	Florian Rousseau (FRA) 0:11.020 min	
Olympic sprint	N/A	N/A	Australia	Great Britain	France 0:44.233 min	
Sprint	Curtis Hartnett (CAN) 0:09.865	Gary Neiwand (AUS) 0:10.129	Jens Fiedler (GER)	Florian Rousseau (FRA)	Marty Nothstein (USA)	OR
Women						
500 m Time trial	Felicia Ballanger (FRA) 0:34.010	Felicia Ballanger (FRA) 0:34.140	Cuihua Jiang (CHN)	Michelle Ferris (AUS)	Felicia Ballanger (FRA) 0:34.140 min	OR
Points race		United States of America	Olga Slioussareva (RUS)	Leontien Zijlaard (NED)	Antonella Bellutti (ITA) 19 pts	
Individual pursuit	Marion Clignet (FRA) 3:30.974	Antonia Bellutti (ITA) 3:32.371	Yvonne McGregor (GBR)	Marion Clignet (FRA)	Leontien Zijlaard (NED) 3:33.360	
Sprint	Olga Slioussareva (URS) 0:10.831	Michelle Ferris (AUS) 0:11.212	Iryna Yanovych (UKR)	Oxana Grichina (RUS)	Felicia Ballanger (FRA)	

Equestrian Dressage, Jumping, Three Day Event

Dressage

Event	1996 Gold Medal Winner	Bronze	Silver	Gold (pts)
Individual	Isabell Werth (GER)	Ulla Salzgeber (GER)	Isabell Werth (GER)	Anky van Grunsven (NED) 239.18
Team	Germany	United States of America	Netherlands	Germany 5632

Jumping

Event	1996 Gold Medal Winner	Bronze	Silver	Gold (pts)
Individual	Ulrich Kirchhoff (GER)	Khaled Al Eid (KSA)	Albert Voorn (NED)	Jeroen Dubbeldam (NED) 4.00
Team	Germany	Brazil	Switzerland	Germany 15.00

Equestrian (cont'd)

Three Day Event

Event	1996 Gold Medal Winner	Bronze	Silver	Gold (pts)
Individual	Blyth Tait (NZL)	Mark Todd (NZL)	Andrew Hoy (AUS)	David O'Connor (USA) 34
Team	Australia	United States of America	Great Britain	Australia 146.80

Fencing

Event	1996 Gold Medal Winner	Bronze	Silver	Gold (pts)
Men				
Épée (Indiv.)	Alexander Beketov (RUS)	Sang-Ki Lee (KOR)	Hugues Obry (FRA)	Pavel Kolobkov (RUS) 15
Épée (Team)	Italy	Cuba	France	Italy 39
Foil (Indiv.)	Alessandro Puccini (ITA)	Dmitri Chevtchenko (RUS)	Ralf Bissdorf (GER)	Young-Ho Kim (KOR) 15
Foil (Team)	Russia	Italy	People's Republic of China	France 45
Sabre (Indiv.)	Stanislav Pozdnyakov (RUS)	Wiradech Kothny (GER)	Mathieu Gourdain (FRA)	Mihai Claudiu Covaliu (ROM) 15
Sabre (Team)	Russia	Germany	France	Russian Federation 45
Women				
Épée (Indiv.)	Laura Flessel (FRA)	Laura Flessel-Colovic (FRA)	Gianna Habluetzel-Buerki (SUI)	Timea Nagy (HUN) 15
Épée (Team)	France	People's Republic of China	Switzerland	Russian Federation 45
Foil (Indiv.)	Laura Badea (ROM)	Giovanna Trillini (ITA)	Rita Koenig (GER)	Valentina Vezzali (ITA) 15
Foil (Team)	Italy	Germany	Poland	Italy 45

Football

Event	1996 Gold Medal Winner	Bronze	Silver	Gold
Men				
	Nigeria	Chile	Spain	Cameroon
Women				
	United States of America	Germany	United States of America	Norway

Gymnastics Artistic, Rhythmic, Trampoline

Artistic

Men

Event	1996 Gold Medal Winner	Bronze	Silver	Gold (pts)
Individual all-around	Li Xiaoshuang (CHN)	Oleksandr Beresh (UKR)	Yang Wei (CHN)	Alexei Nemov (RUS) 58.474
Team	Russian Federation	Russian Federation	Ukraine	People's Republic of China 231.919
Floor	Ioannis Melissanidis (GRE)	Iordan Iovtchev (BUL)	Alexei Nemov (RUS)	Igors Vihrovs (LAT) 9.812
Horizontal bar	Andreas Wecker (GER)	Joo-Hyung Lee (KOR)	Benjamin Varonian (FRA)	Alexei Nemov (RUS) 9.787
Parallel bars	Rustam Sharipov (UKR)	Alexei Nemov (RUS)	Joo-Hyung Lee (KOR)	Li Xiaopeng (CHN) 9.825
Pommel	Li Donghua (SUI)	Alexei Nemov (RUS)	Eric Poujade (FRA)	Marius Urzica (ROM) 9.862
Rings	Yuri Chechi (ITA)	Iordan Iovtchev (BUL)	Dimosthenis Tampakos (GRE)	Szilveszter Csollany (HUN) 9.850
Vault	Alexei Nemov (RUS)	Leszek Blanik (POL)	Alexey Bondarenko (RUS)	Gervasio Deferr (ESP) 9.712

Women

Event	1996 Gold Medal Winner	Bronze	Silver	Gold (pts)
Individual all-around	Lilia Podkopayeva (UKR)	Liu Xuan (CHN)	Maria Olaru (ROM)	Simona Amanar (ROM) 38.642
Team	United States of America	People's Republic of China	Russian Federation	Romania 154.608
Beam	Shannon Miller (USA)	Elena Produnova (RUS)	Ekaterina Lobazniouk (RUS)	Liu Xuan (CHN) 9.825
Floor	Lilia Podkopayeva (UKR)	Simona Amanar (ROM)	Svetlana Khorkina (RUS)	Elena Zamolodtchikova (RUS) 9.850
Uneven bars	Svetlana Chorkina (RUS)	Yang Yun (CHN)	Ling Jie (CHN)	Svetlana Khorkina (RUS) 9.862
Vault	Simona Amanar (ROM)	Ekaterina Lobazniouk (RUS)	Andreea Raducan (ROM)	Elena Zamolodtchikova (RUS) 9.731

Rhythmic

Event	1996 Gold Medal Winner	Bronze	Silver	Gold (pts)
Group competition	Spain	Greece	Belarus	Russian Federation 39.500
Individual competition	Yekaterina Serebryanskaya (UKR)	Alina Kabaeva (RUS)	Yulia Raskina (BLR)	Yulia Barsukova (RUS) 39.632

Trampoline

Event	1996 Gold Medal Winner	Bronze	Silver	Gold (pts)
Men				
	New event	Mathieu Turgeon (CAN)	Ji Wallace (AUS)	Alexandre Moskalenko (RUS) 41.70
Women				
	New event	Karen Cockburn (CAN)	Oxana Tsyhuleva (UKR)	Irina Karavaeva (RUS) 38.90

Handball

Event	1996 Gold Medal Winner	Bronze	Silver	Gold
Men				
	Croatia	Spain	Sweden	Russian Federation
Women				
	Denmark	Norway	Hungary	Denmark

Hockey

Event	1996 Gold Medal Winner	Bronze	Silver	Gold
Men				
	Netherlands	Australia	Korea	Netherlands
Women				
	Australia	Netherlands	Argentina	Australia

Judo

Event	1996 Gold Medal Winner	Bronze	Silver	Gold
Men				
60 kg	New weight	Manolo Poulot (CUB) & Aidyn Smagulov (KGZ)	Bu-Kyung Jung (KOR)	Tadahiro Nomura (JPN)
66 kg	divisions	Girolamo Giovinazzo (ITA) & Giorgi Vazagashvili (GEO)	Larbi Benboudaoud (FRA)	Huseyin Ozkan (TUR)
73 kg	for 2000	Anatoly Laryukov (BLR) & Vsevolods Zelonijs (LAT)	Tiago Camilo (BRA)	Giuseppe Maddaloni (ITA)
81 kg	Olympic	Aleksei Budolin (EST) & Nuno Delgado (POR)	In-Chul Cho (KOR)	Makoto Takimoto (JPN)

Judo (cont'd)

Event	1996 Gold Medal Winner	Bronze	Silver	Gold
Men				
90 kg	Games	Frederic Demontfaucon (FRA) & Ruslan Mashurenko (UKR)	Carlos Honorato (BRA)	Mark Huizinga (NED)
100 kg		Iouri Stepkine (RUS) & Stephane Traineau (FRA)	Nicolas Gill (CAN)	Kosei Inoue (JPN)
100+ kg		Indrek Pertelson (EST) & Tamerlan Tmenov (RUS)	Shinichi Shinohara (JPN)	David Douillet (FRA)
Women				
48 kg	New weight	Anna-Maria Gradante (GER) & Ann Simons (BEL)	Lioubov Brouletova (RUS)	Ryoko Tamura (JPN)
52 kg	division	Sun Hui Kye (PRK) & Liu Yuxiang (CHN)	Noriko Narazaki (JPN)	Legna Verdecia (CUB)
57 kg	for 2000	Kie Kusakabe (JPN) & Maria Pekli (AUS)	Driulys Gonzalez (CUB)	Isabel Fernandez (ESP)
63 kg	Olympic	Sung-Sook Jung (KOR) & Gella Vandecaveye (BEL)	Li Shufang (CHN)	Severine Vandenhende (FRA)
70 kg	Games	Min-Sun Cho (KOR) & Ylenia Scapin (ITA)	Kate Howey (GBR)	Sibelis Veranes (CUB)
78 kg		Simona Marcela Richter (ROM) & Emanuela Pierantozzi (ITA)	Celine Lebrun (FRA)	Tang Lin (CHN)
78+ kg		Seon-Young Kim (KOR) & Mayumi Yamashita (JPN)	Daima Mayelis Beltran (CUB)	Yuan Hua (CHN)

Modern Pentathlon

Event	1996 Gold Medal Winner	Bronze	Silver	Gold (pts)
Men				
	Alexander Parygin (KAZ)	Pavel Dovgal (BLR)	Gabor Balogh (HUN)	Dmitry Svatkovsky (RUS) 5376
Women				
	New event	Kate Allenby (GBR)	Emily deRiel (USA)	Stephanie Cook (GBR) 5318

Rowing

Event	1996 Gold Medal Winner	Bronze	Silver	Gold (min)
Men				
Single sculls	Xeno Mueller (SUI)	Marcel Hacker (GER)	Xeno Mueller (SUI)	Rob Waddell (NZL) 6:48.90
Double sculls	Italy	Italy	Norway	Slovenia 6:16.63
Lightweight double sculls	Switzerland	France	Italy	Poland 6:21.75
Quadruple sculls	Germany	Germany	Netherlands	Italy 5:45.56
Coxless pair	Great Britain	Australia	United States of America	France 6:32.97

Rowing (cont'd)

Event	1996 Gold Medal Winner	Bronze	Silver	Gold (min)
Men				
Coxless four	Australia	Australia	Italy	Great Britain 5:56.24
Lightweight coxless four	Denmark	Denmark	Australia	France 6:01.68
Eight	Netherlands	Croatia	Australia	Great Britain 5:33.08
Women				
Single sculls	Yekaterina Khodotovich (BLR)	Katrin Rutschow-Stomporowski (GER)	Rumyana Neykova (BUL)	Ekaterina Karsten (BLR) 7:28.14
Double sculls	Canada	Lithuania	Netherlands	Germany 6:55.44
Lightweight double sculls	Romania	United States of America	Germany	Romania 7:02.64
Quadruple sculls	Germany	Russian Federation	Great Britain	Germany 6:19.58
Coxless pair	Australia	United States of America	Australia	Romania 7:11.00
Eight	Romania	Canada	Netherlands	Romania 6:06.44

Sailing

Event	1996 Gold Medal Winner	Bronze	Silver	Gold (pts)
Men				
Mistral	Nikolas Kaklamanakis (GRE)	Aaron McIntosh (NZL)	Carlos Espinola (ARG)	Christoph Sieber (AUT) 38
Finn	Mateusz Kusnierewicz (POL)	Fredrik Loof (SWE)	Luca Devoti (ITA)	Iain Percy (GBR) 35
470	Ukraine	Argentina	United States of America	Australia 38
Women				
Mistral	Lai-Shan Lee (HKG)	Barbara Kendall (NZL)	Amelie Lux (GER)	Alessandra Sensini (ITA) 15
Europe	Kristine Roug (DEN)	Serena Amato (ARG)	Margriet Matthysse (NED)	Shirley Robertson (GBR) 37
470	Spain	Ukraine	United States of America	Australia 33
Open				
Laser	Robert Scheidt (BRA)	Michael Blackburn (AUS)	Robert Scheidt (BRA)	Ben Ainslie (GBR) 42
Tornado	Spain	Germany	Australia	Austria 16
Star	Brazil	Brazil	Great Britain	United States of America 34
49er	New event	United States of America	Great Britain	Finland 55
Soling	Germany	Norway	Germany	Denmark

Current Records as at 01/10/2000

New Record

Men

Event	World Record (pts)	Olympic Record (pts)	Bronze	Silver	Gold (pts)	WR/OR
10 m Air rifle	Jason Parker (USA) 700.6	Cai Yalin (CHN) 696.4	Evgueni Aleinikov (RUS)	Artem Khajibekov (RUS)	Cai Yalin (CHN) 696.4	OR
50 m Free rifle prone	Christian Klees (GER) 704.8	Christian Klees (GER) 704.8	Sergei Martynov (BLR)	Torben Grimmel (DEN)	Jonas Edman (SWE) 701.3	
50 m Free rifle 3x40	Rajmond Debevec (SLO) 1287.9	Rajmond Debevec (SLO) 1275.1	Harald Stenvaag (NOR)	Juha Hirvi (FIN)	Rajmond Debevec (SLO) 1275.1	OR
10 m Air pistol	Sergei Pyzhianov (URS) 695.1	Franck Dumoulin (FRA) 688.9	Igor Basinsky (BLR)	Wang Yifu (CHN)	Franck Dumoulin (FRA) 688.9	OR
25 m Rapid fire pistol	Ralf Schumann (GER) 699.7	Ralf Schumann (GER) 698.0	Iulian Raicea (ROM)	Michel Ansermet (SUI)	Serguei Alifirenko (RUS) 687.6	
50 m Free pistol	William Damarest (USA) 676.2	Boris Kokorev (RUS) 666.4	Martin Tenk (CZE)	Igor Basinsky (BLR)	Tanyu Kiriakov (BUL) 666.0	
10 m Running target	Yang Ling (CHN) 687.9	Yang Ling (CHN) 686.8	Niu Zhiyuan (CHN)	Oleg Moldovan (MDA)	Yang Ling (CHN) 681.1	
Trap	Marcello Tittarelli (ITA) 150.0	Michael Diamond (AUS) 149.0	Giovanni Pellielo (ITA)	Ian Peel (GBR)	Michael Diamond (AUS) 147.0	
Double trap	Daniele Di Spigno (ITA) 194.0	Russell Mark (AUS) 189.0	Fehaid Al Deehani (KUW)	Russell Mark (AUS)	Richard Faulds (GBR) 187.0	
Skeet	Harald Jensen (NOR), Ennio Falco (ITA), Andrea Benelli (ITA), Jan Henrik Heinrich (GER), Franck Durbesson (FRA) & Mykola Milchev (UKR) 150.0	Mykola Milchev (UKR) 150.0	James Graves (USA)	Petr Malek (CZE)	Mykola Milchev (UKR) 150.0	WR OR

Women

Event	World Record (pts)	Olympic Record (pts)	Bronze	Silver	Gold (pts)	WR/OR
10 m Air rifle	Gaby Buehlmann (SUI) 503.5	Kab Soon Yeo (KOR) 498.2	Gao Jing (CHN)	Cho-Hyun Kang (KOR)	Nancy Johnson (USA) 497.7	
50 m Sport rifle 3x20	Wang Xian (CHN) 689.7	Alexandra Ivosev (YUG) 686.1	Maria Feklistova (RUS)	Tatiana Goldobina (RUS)	Renata Mauer-Rozanska (POL) 684.6	
10 m Air pistol	Ren Jie (CHN) 493.5	Olga Klochneva (RUS) 490.1	Annemarie Forder (AUS)	Jasna Sekaric (YUG)	Tao Luna (CHN) 488.2	
25 m Pistol	Diana Jorgova (BUL) 696.2	Maria Grozdeva (BUL) 690.3	Lolita Evglevskaya (BLR)	Tao Luna (CHN)	Maria Grozdeva (BUL) 690.3	OR
Trap	Satu Pusila (FIN) & Delphine Racinet (FRA) 95.0	Diana Gudzineviciute (LTU) 93.0	Gao E (CHN)	Delphine Racinet (FRA)	Diana Gudzineviciute (LTU) 93.0	OR
Double trap	Deborah Gelisio (ITA) 149.0	Pia Hansen (SWE) 148.0	Kimberly Rhode (USA)	Deborah Gelisio (ITA)	Pia Hansen (SWE) 148.0	OR
Skeet	Svetlana Demina (RUS) 99.0	Zemfira Meftakhetdinova (AZE)	Diana Igaly (HUN)	Svetlana Demina (RUS)	Zemfira Meftakhetdinova (AZE) 98.0	OR

Softball

Event	1996 Gold Medal Winner	Bronze	Silver	Gold
Women	United States of America	Australia	Japan	United States of America

Table Tennis

Event	1996 Gold Medal Winner	Bronze	Silver	Gold
Men				
Singles	Liu Guoliang (CHN)	Lin Guoliang (CHN)	Jan-Ove Waldner (SWE)	Kong Linghui (CHN)
Doubles	People's Republic of China	France	People's Republic of China	People's Republic of China
Women				
Singles	Deng Yaping (CHN)	Jing Chen (TPE)	Li Ju (CHN)	Wang Nan (CHN)
Doubles	People's Republic of China	Korea	People's Republic of China	People's Republic of China

Taekwondo

Event	1996 Gold Medal Winner	Bronze	Silver	Gold
Men				
Less than 58 kg	New	Chih-Hsiung Huang (TPE)	Gabriel Esparza (ESP)	Michail Mouroutsos (GRE)
58 kg–68 kg	Olympic	Hadi Saeibonehkohai (IRI)	Joon-Sik Sin (KOR)	Steven Lopez (USA)
68 kg–80 kg	Sport	Victor Manuel Estrada Garibay (MEX)	Faissal Ebnoutalib (GER)	Angel Valodia Matos Fuentes (CUB)
80+ kg		Pascal Gentil (FRA)	Daniel Trenton (AUS)	Kyong-Hun Kim (KOR)
Women				
Less than 49 kg	New	Shu-Ju Chi (TPE)	Urbia Melendez Rodriguez (CUB)	Lauren Burns (AUS)
49 kg–57 kg	Olympic	Hamide Bikcin (TUR)	Hieu Ngan Tran (VIE)	Jae-Eun Jung (KOR)
57 kg–67 kg	Sport	Yoriko Okamoto (JPN)	Trude Gundersen (NOR)	Sun-Hee Lee (KOR)
67+ kg		Dominique Bosshart (CAN)	Natalia Ivanova (RUS)	Chen Zhong (CHN)

Tennis

Event	1996 Gold Medal Winner	Bronze	Silver	Gold
Men				
Singles	Andre Agassi (USA)	Arnaud di Pasquale (FRA)	Tommy Haas (GER)	Yevgeny Kafelnikov (RUS)
Doubles	Australia	Spain	Australia	Canada
Women				
Singles	Lindsay Davenport (USA)	Monica Seles (USA)	Elena Dementieva (RUS)	Venus Williams (USA)
Doubles	United States of America	Belgium	Netherlands	United States of America

Triathlon

Event	1996 Gold Medal Winner	Bronze	Silver	Gold (min)
Men	New Olympic sport	Jan Rehula (CZE)	Stephan Vuckovic (GER)	Simon Whitfield (CAN) 1:48:24.02
Women	New Olympic sport	Magali Messmer (SUI)	Michellie Jones (AUS)	Brigitte McMahon (SUI) 2:00:40.52

Volleyball Beach Volleyball, Volleyball

Beach Volleyball

Event	1996 Gold Medal Winner	Bronze	Silver	Gold
Men	United States of America	Germany	Brazil	United States of America
Women	Brazil	Brazil	Brazil	Australia

Volleyball

Event	1996 Gold Medal Winner	Bronze	Silver	Gold
Men	Netherlands	Italy	Russian Federation	Yugoslavia
Women	Cuba	Brazil	Russian Federation	Cuba

Weightlifting

Current Records as at 01/10/2000

Event	World Record (kg)	Olympic Record (kg)	Bronze	Silver	Gold (kg)	WR/OR
Men						
56 kg	Halil Mutlu (TUR) 305.0	Halil Mutlu (TUR) 305.0	Zhang Xiangxiang (CHN)	Wu Wenxiong (CHN)	Halil Mutlu (TUR) 305.0	WR OR
62 kg	*	Nikolay Pechalov (CRO) 325.0	Gennady Oleshchuk (BLR)	Leonidas Sabanis (GRE)	Nikolay Pechalov (CRO) 325.0	OR
69 kg	Galabin Boevski (BUL) 357.5	Galabin Boevski (BUL) 357.5	Sergei Lavrenov (BLR)	Georgi Markov (BUL)	Galabin Boevski (BUL) 357.5	OR
77 kg	*	*	Arsen Melikyan (ARM)	Viktor Mitrou (GRE)	Zhan Xugang (CHN) 367.5	
85 kg	*	*	George Asanidze (GEO)	Marc Huster (GER)	Pyrros Dimas (GRE) 390.0	
94 kg	*	*	Alexei Petrov (RUS)	Szymon Kolecki (POL)	Akakios Kakiasvilis (GRE) 405.0	
105 kg	*	*	Said S Asaad (QAT)	Alan Tsagaev (BUL)	Hossein Tavakoli (IRI) 425.0	
105+ kg	Hossein Rezazadeh (IRI) 472.5	Hossein Rezazadeh (IRI) 472.5	Andrei Chemerkin (RUS)	Ronny Weller (GER)	Hossein Rezazadeh (IRI) 472.5	WR OR
Women						
48 kg	Li Xiuhua (CHN) 197.5	*	Sri Indriyani (INA)	Raema Lisa Rumbewas (INA)	Tara Nott (USA) 185.0	
53 kg	Yang Xia (CHN) 225.0	Yang Xia (CHN) 225.0	Winami Binti Slamet (INA)	Feng-Ying Li (TPE)	Yang Xia (CHN) 225.0	WR OR
58 kg	Chen Yanqing (CHN) 235.0	*	Khassaraporn Suta (THA)	Song Hui Ri (PRK)	Soraya Jimenez Mendivil (MEX) 222.5	
63 kg	Chen Xiaomin (CHN) 242.5	Chen Xiaomin (CHN) 242.5	Ioanna Chatziioannou (GRE)	Valentina Popova (RUS)	Chen Xiaomin (CHN) 242.5	WR OR
69 kg	Lin Weining (CHN) 252.5	*	Karnam Malleswari (IND)	Erzsebet Markus (HUN)	Lin Weining (CHN) 242.5	
75 kg	Sun Tianni (CHN) 257.5	*	Yi-Hang Kuo (TPE)	Ruth Ogbeifo (NGR)	Maria Isabel Urrutia (COL) 245.0	
75+ kg	Ding Meiyuan (CHN) 300.0	Ding Meiyuan (CHN) 300.0	Cheryl Haworth (USA)	Agata Wrobel (POL)	Ding Meiyuan (CHN) 300.0	WR OR

* The minimum weight for World or Olympic Record recognition has not been achieved yet. Note: Records are combined scores of the Snatch and Clean and Jerk.

Wrestling Freestyle, Greco-Roman

Freestyle

Event	1996 Gold Medal Winner	Bronze	Silver	Gold
54 kg	New	Amiran Karritanov (GRE)	Samuel Henson (USA)	Namig Abdullayev (AZE)
58 kg	weight	Terry Brands (USA)	Yevgen Buslovych (UKR)	Alireza Dabir (IRI)
63 kg	divisions	Jae Sung Jang (KOR)	Serafim Barzakov (BUL)	Mourad Oumakhanov (RUS)
69 kg	for 2000	Lincoln McIlravy (USA)	Arsen Gitinov (RUS)	Daniel Igali (CAN)
76 kg	Olympic	Eri Jae Moon (KOR)	Brandon Slay (USA)	Alexander Leipold (GER)
85 kg	Games	Mogamed Ibragimov (MKD)	Yoel Romero (CUB)	Adam Saitiev (RUS)
97 kg		Eldar Kurtanidze (GEO)	Islam Bairamukov (KAZ)	Saghid Mourtsaliyev (RUS)
130 kg		Alexis Rodriguez (CUB)	Artur Taymazov (UZB)	David Moussoulbes (RUS)

Greco–Roman

Event	1996 Gold Medal Winner	Bronze	Silver	Gold
54 kg		Yong Gyun Kang (PRK)	Lazaro Rivas (CUB)	Kwon Ho Sim (KOR)
58 kg	New	Sheng Zetian (CHN)	In-Sub Kim (KOR)	Armen Nazarian (BUL)
63 kg	weight	Akaki Chachua (GEO)	Juan Luis Maren (CUB)	Varteres Samourgachev (RUS)
69 kg	divisions	Alexei Glouchkov (RUS)	Katsuhiko Nagata (JPN)	Filiberto Azcuy (CUB)
76 kg	for 2000	Marko Yli-Hannuksela (FIN)	Matt James Lindland (USA)	Mourat Kardanov (RUS)
85 kg	Olympic	Mukhran Vakhtangadze (GEO)	Sandor Istvan Bardosi (HUN)	Hamza Yerlikaya (TUR)
97 kg	Games	Garrett Lowney (USA)	Davyd Saldadze (UKR)	Mikael Ljungberg (SWE)
130 kg		Dmitry Debelka (BLR)	Alexandre Kareline (RUS)	Rulon Gardner (USA)

Nation abbreviations

AHO	Netherlands Antilles	CYP	Cyprus
ALB	Albania	CZE	Czech Republic
ALG	Algeria	DEN	Denmark
AND	Andorra	DJI	Djibouti
ANG	Angola	DMA	Dominica
ANT	Antigua and Barbuda	DOM	Dominican Republic
		ECU	Ecuador
ARG	Argentina	EGY	Egypt
ARM	Armenia	ERI	Eritrea
ARU	Aruba	ESA	El Salvador
ASA	American Samoa	ESP	Spain
AUS	Australia	EST	Estonia
AUT	Austria	ETH	Ethiopia
AZE	Azerbaijan	FIJ	Fiji
BAH	Bahamas	FIN	Finland
BAN	Bangladesh	FRA	France
BAR	Barbados	FSM	Federated States of Micronesia
BDI	Burundi		
BEL	Belgium	GAB	Gabon
BEN	Benin	GAM	Gambia
BER	Bermuda	GBR	Great Britain
BHU	Bhutan	GBS	Guinea–Bissau
BIH	Bosnia and Herzegovina	*GDR*	*East Germany (1949–1990)*
BIZ	Belize	GEO	Georgia
BLR	Belarus	GEQ	Equatorial Guinea
BOL	Bolivia	GER	Germany
BOT	Botswana	GHA	Ghana
BRA	Brazil	GRE	Greece
BRN	Bahrain	GRN	Grenada
BRU	Brunei Darussalam	GUA	Guatemala
BUL	Bulgaria	GUI	Guinea
BUR	Burkina Faso	GUM	Guam
CAF	Central African Republic	GUY	Guyana
		HAI	Haiti
CAM	Cambodia	HKG	Hong Kong, China
CAN	Canada	HON	Honduras
CAY	Cayman Islands	HUN	Hungary
CGO	Congo	INA	Indonesia
CHA	Chad	IND	India
CHI	Chile	IRI	Islamic Republic of Iran
CHN	People's Republic of China		
		IRL	Ireland
CIS	*Commonwealth of Independent States, 1992*	IRQ	Iraq
		ISL	Iceland
		ISR	Israel
CIV	Côte d'Ivoire	ISV	Virgin Islands
CMR	Cameroon	ITA	Italy
COD	Democratic Republic of the Congo	IVB	British Virgin Islands
		JAM	Jamaica
COK	Cook Islands	JOR	Jordan
COL	Colombia	JPN	Japan
COM	Comoros	KAZ	Kazakstan
CPV	Cape Verde	KEN	Kenya
CRC	Costa Rica	KGZ	Kyrgyzstan
CRO	Croatia	KOR	Korea
CUB	Cuba	KSA	Saudi Arabia
KUW	Kuwait	RSA	South Africa
LAO	Lao People's Democratic Republic	RUS	Russian Federation
		RWA	Rwanda
LAT	Latvia	SAM	Samoa
LBA	Libyan Arab Jamahiriya	SEN	Senegal
		SEY	Seychelles
LBR	Liberia	SIN	Singapore
LCA	Saint Lucia	SKN	Saint Kitts and Nevis
LES	Lesotho		
LIB	Lebanon	SLE	Sierra Leone
LIE	Liechtenstein	SLO	Slovenia
LTU	Lithuania	SMR	San Marino
LUX	Luxembourg	SOL	Solomon Islands
MAD	Madagascar	SOM	Somalia
MAR	Morocco	SRI	Sri Lanka
MAS	Malaysia	STP	Sao Tome and Principe
MAW	Malawi		
MDA	Republic of Moldova	SUD	Sudan
MDV	Maldives	SUI	Switzerland
MEX	Mexico	SUR	Suriname
MGL	Mongolia	SVK	Slovakia
MKD	Former Yugoslav Republic of Macedonia	SWE	Sweden
		SWZ	Swaziland
		SYR	Syrian Arab Republic
MLI	Mali		
MLT	Malta	TAN	United Republic of Tanzania
MON	Monaco		
MOZ	Mozambique	*TCH*	*Czechoslovakia (to 1993)*
MRI	Mauritius		
MTN	Mauritania	TGA	Tonga
MYA	Myanmar	THA	Thailand
NAM	Namibia	TJK	Tajikistan
NCA	Nicaragua	TKM	Turkmenistan
NED	Netherlands	TOG	Togo
NEP	Nepal	TPE	Chinese Taipei
NGR	Nigeria	TRI	Trinidad and Tobago
NIG	Niger	TUN	Tunisia
NOR	Norway	TUR	Turkey
NRU	Nauru	UAE	United Arab Emirates
NZL	New Zealand		
OMA	Oman	UGA	Uganda
PAK	Pakistan	UKR	Ukraine
PAN	Panama	*URS*	*Soviet Union (to 1992)*
PAR	Paraguay		
PER	Peru	URU	Uruguay
PHI	Philippines	USA	United States of America
PLE	Palestine		
PLW	Palau	UZB	Uzbekistan
PNG	Papua New Guinea	VAN	Vanuatu
POL	Poland	VEN	Venezuela
POR	Portugal	VIE	Vietnam
PRK	Democratic People's Republic of Korea	VIN	Saint Vincent and the Grenadines
		YEM	Yemen
PUR	Puerto Rico	YUG	Yugoslavia
QAT	Qatar	ZAM	Zambia
ROM	Romania	ZIM	Zimbabwe

Penguin Books Ltd, Melbourne, London, New York, Toronto, Auckland,
South Africa, India

First published by Penguin Books Australia, 2000
This edition © Penguin Books Australia Ltd
487 Maroondah Highway, PO Box 257
Ringwood, Victoria 3134, Australia

TM © SOCOG 1996

The publishers have made every effort to ensure that the
information in this book was correct at the time of publication.

SOCOG has authorised and approved the information in this book.

National Library of Australia
Cataloguing-in-Publication data:

The winners Sydney 2000 Olympic Games

ISBN 0 14 100027 9.

1. Olympic Games (27th :, 2000 : Sydney, N.S.W.).
2. Olympics - Records. 3. Olympics - History.

796.48

Sports reports by Murray Olds
Writers: John Ross and Evan McHugh
Editorial management and copy-editing: Astrid Browne,
Wendy Skilbeck and Susan McLeish
Editorial assistance: Saskia Adams, Michael Archer,
Lynda Fittolani, Heidi Marfurt and Julie Sheridan
Designed by John Canty and Marta White with assistance from
Susannah Low, Penguin Design Studio
Cover design by David Altheim, Penguin Design Studio

Printed and bound in Australia through
australian book connection, Victoria

ACKNOWLEDGEMENTS
Front cover photographs:
Left (Cathy Freeman): Stu Forster/Allsport
Centre (Ian Thorpe): Al Bello/Allsport
Right (Andrew Hoy): Al Bello/Allsport
Back cover photographs:
Medals: © IOC/Olympic Museum Collection
Top, left (Grant Hackett): Hamish Blair/Allsport
Top, centre (Simone Hankin): Scott Barbour/Allsport
Top, right (Inge de Bruijn): Ross Kinnaird/Allsport
Bottom, left (Marion Jones): Mike Powell/Allsport
Bottom, centre (Brett Aitken and Scott McGrory): Mike Powell/Allsport
Bottom, right (Simon Fairweather): Hamish Blair/Allsport
Text photographs: Allsport
Photograph of Opening Ceremony (top, p. 4):
TRENT PARKE/COURTESY OF THE AGE
Stamps of Olympic gold medal winners (p. 86): Australia Post